THE BATTLE OF
MIDWAY

THE BATTLE OF
MIDWAY
PETER C. SMITH

NEW ENGLISH LIBRARY
TIMES MIRROR

A New English Library Original Publication 1976
© by Peter C. Smith, 1976

*

FIRST NEL PAPERBACK EDITION AUGUST 1976

*

NEL Books are published by
New English Library Limited from Barnard's Inn, Holborn, London EC1N 2JR
Made and printed in Great Britain by Hunt Barnard Printing Ltd., Aylesbury, Bucks.

45002930 1

CONTENTS

AUTHOR'S NOTE

It is doubtful whether the full and complete story of the Battle of Midway will ever be told. Such is the complexity of modern warfare, especially sea/air warfare. Midway was a confusing battle and despite the enormous flood of writings on it many points of detail remain open to differing interpretations.

The most valid and useful source material still remains the file at the Public Record Office, in London (ADM 199/1302); Professor Samuel Eliot Morison's *History of United States Naval Operations in World War II*, Volume IV, *Coral Sea, Midway and Submarine Actions*, (OUP 1949); and *Midway: The Battle that Doomed Japan*, by Mitsuo Fuchida and Masatake Okumiya (Hutchinson, 1957). The general reader is therefore recommended to turn first to these sources on completion of this book.

Peter C. Smith   Needingworth, Cambs.

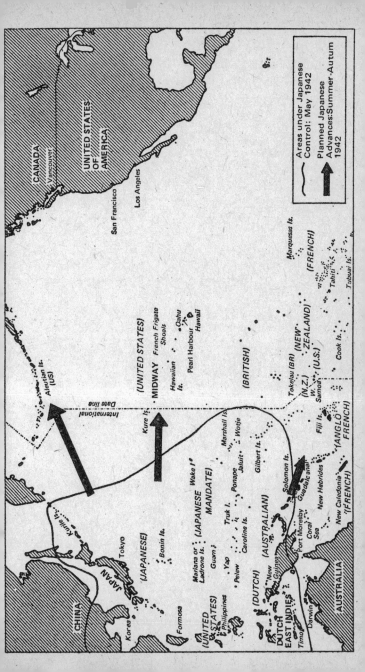

CHAPTER ONE

THE SLEDGEHAMMER

On 17 March 1924, the Director of War Plans at the American Navy Department made a prediction:

'The importance of the use of aircraft in a Pacific campaign promises to be such that every effort should be made to attain and maintain an advantage in this respect. This is of particular importance, because Japanese aircraft can operate in the probable theatre of operations from shore bases; whereas our aircraft must operate from carriers in the initial stages of the campaign.'

But seventeen years later the Japanese had carriers also ...

At 0800 on a calm and peaceful Sunday morning on 7 December 1941, the great battleships of the American Pacific Fleet lay slumbering at their moorings at Pearl Harbor in the Hawaii Islands. The huge ships lay in pairs, the very symbol of American naval might and power, their great batteries of heavy guns the very epitome of supreme confidence and overwhelming strength.

On the deck of the old mine-layer *Oglala* Rear Admiral W. R. Furlong glanced up as a flight of nine aircraft passed swiftly over towards Ford Island in the centre of the anchorage. A huge explosion blasted the still morning air.

High above the anchorage Commander Mitsuo Fuchida of the Imperial Japanese Navy looked down on the carnage below as plane after plane of the Japanese strike force peeled off towards their targets almost unopposed. Surprise was complete. He signalled immediately to his commander, Admiral Chuichi Nagumo, waiting aboard the aircraft-carrier flagship *Akagi* some 200 miles out to sea, '*Tora, tora, tora*'. A new era in naval warfare had burst upon the world.

An hour later, the waters of Pearl Harbor were filled with burning and sinking ships. The battleship *Arizona* had blown up with appalling loss of life, while most of her sisters were ablaze or listing from torpedo hits. Ashore, smoke rose in great columns from the rows of burnt-out fighter and bomber aircraft blazing on their home airfields.

The carrier had come of age.

Admiral Sir Tom Phillips of the Royal Navy was a brave, intelligent and courageous officer, a typical product of his era. Before the war he shared a flat in London with John Slessor, later to become Marshal of the Royal Air Force, but the two, although firm friends, could never agree on the ability of a bomber to hit, let alone sink, a battleship. When Phillips was promoted and left the planning staff, Bert Harris, later Marshal of the Royal Air Force where he was known as Sir Arthur 'Bomber' Harris, proposed a farewell toast at a goodbye party.

'Tom,' he said, 'when the first bomb hits, you'll say, "My God, what a hell of a mine!"'

But Admiral Phillips maintained his faith in his anti-aircraft guns and armoured decks. On 10 December 1941, just three days after Pearl Harbor, he was in command of the powerful Force 'Z' based at Singapore with the battleship *Prince of Wales* and the old battle-cruiser *Repulse*. When reports came in of a Japanese landing fleet off the coast he unhesitatingly put to sea to destroy it.

As the great ships steamed towards the enemy, reported to be protected by two Japanese battleships, a signal was received by the Air Officer Commanding, Malaya. No fighters could be expected over the area of operations, it read, due to the fact that the RAF had been forced to pull back its aircraft due to heavy bombing. Admiral Phillips shrugged his shoulders.

'Well,' he said, 'we must get on without it.'

At 1100 on the 10th a formation of nine high-altitude bombers was sighted approaching the fleet at 10,000 feet. The anti-aircraft guns started to boom in defiance but the Japanese Navy pilots held their formation and released their bombs. Great geysers of spray shot up around the *Repulse* as the first

12

heavy bomb plunged through the hangar and hit the armoured deck. The first direct hit had fallen and there was more to come.

Wave after wave of the Japanese bombers came on, torpedo-bombers and altitude attacks followed each other with rapidity and precision. An hour and a half after the first attack, the *Repulse* had been hit by no less than five torpedoes and rolled over and sank. Less than an hour later the *Prince of Wales* which had been hit by six torpedoes and one bomb also rolled over and followed the *Repulse* to the bottom, taking Tom Phillips and over three hundred of her crew with her.

It was in the late 1930s that a sleek and powerful heavy cruiser of the Royal Navy lay at anchor in a North American port. She was on a courtesy visit and her decks were thronged with guests all eagerly inspecting this representative of His Majesty's Fleet. She was a 'County' class cruiser, the largest in the Royal Navy and she mounted eight of the new 8in guns in four twin turrets fore and aft.

It was a particularly special occasion for two men that day, one a torpedo petty officer of the ship and the other a visitor. They were brothers who had not met for a dozen years. One had joined the Royal Navy as a boy seaman, the other had 'gone to the colonies', had emigrated to Canada as a lad and had worked in near slave-like conditions for a farmer ever since. Their reunion was a joyful occasion but after a while their conversation turned to more sombre topics, the imminence of war.

Both were patriots who firmly believed that sooner or later Britain would have to stand up to the dictators of both east and west, they had no illusions on that score. The sailor was confident and pointed out to his brother the equipment his ship would use to deal with any enemy heavy cruiser. 'But what of aircraft?' asked his brother. He was led amidships and proudly shown the skyward-pointing muzzles of the four twin 4in guns and the multiple machine-gun nests. 'And here,' said the sailor, 'look at these. They are multiple pom-poms, automatic weapons that we call "Chicago pianos". They can throw up a steel curtain of exploding 2 pounder shells over the ship that no aircraft can ever penetrate.'

The Canadian went away deeply impressed, not only at the state of the Royal Navy and its readiness, but at its quiet confidence in its ability to deal with any enemy. And this feeling was shared by others, countless thousands in the Empire, Canada, Malaya, India and in Australia, the Navy was still 'the sure shield' against any potential enemy . . .

It was April 1942, and the azure blue depths of the calm and tranquil waters of the Indian Ocean were cut by a pair of long lazy white wakes. Across the gentle ocean steamed two 'County' class heavy cruisers, *Dorsetshire* and *Cornwall.* They had been detached from Admiral Somerville's main fleet even though there were rumours of a Japanese carrier task force operating in the area. But in three years of warfare the two ships had shown their strength in dealing with enemy surface raiders, blockade runners and the like and their confidence was high.

Aboard the *Akagi* Admiral Nagumo received a sighting report from one of his search planes: 'Two enemy heavy cruisers sighted heading south.'

Immediately, from the decks of the Japanese carriers, there arose a swarm of sparkling Hornets, the eighty Val dive-bombers of Lieutenant Commander Egusa's strike force. They droned off into the clear sky towards the last reported position of the two cruisers.

At 1400 Admiral Somerville's fleet received a highly garbled and brief radio signal from the *Dorsetshire* mentioning a shadowing aircraft and soon afterwards the radar screens on Somerville's flagship showed a large formation of aircraft on *Dorsetshire*'s bearing. Nothing more was heard from the two cruisers but an hour later a scouting plane reported a large amount of floating debris and wreckage and many men in the water in the cruisers' last known position.

Nagumo also had received no further news until suddenly he received from Egusa the message, 'Enemy sighted.'

Twenty minutes later it was all over and both cruisers, 'those dignified symbols of an obsolete Pax Britannica', had been sunk.

Commander Fuchida was to later recall that: 'The dive-bombers scored hits with close to ninety per cent of their bombs

– an enviable rate of accuracy, even considering the windless conditions. But rather than feeling exultation over the proficiency of Egusa's bombardiers, I could only feel pity for these surface ships assailed from the air at odds of forty to one.'

Thus, after less than six months of war with the Japanese Navy it had come to this. The derided and scorned Oriental opponent who, it was claimed, was almost blind, flew cardboard planes and was armed with only a samurai sword, had not only slaughtered his mighty opponents' fleets with childish ease and speed, but was moved to pity at the pathetic state of the defences he had encountered in doing so.

How could it be that the flyers of the Imperial Japanese Navy could achieve all this with negligible losses? For had not magazines like *Aviation* assured their public that ' . . . the chief military airplanes of Japan are either outdated already or are becoming outdated . . . '

In the early summer months of 1942 the men of the Imperial Japanese Navy could look back on six months of victorious combat unequalled in the annals of their nation. From the first carrier-launched attack on the anchored battleships of the slumbering American fleet at Pearl Harbor on 7 December 1941, to the landing of their troops at Tulagi, in the Solomon Islands, their ships and aircraft had swept all before them while their dogged infantrymen had occupied, with comparative ease, a whole string of military bastions formerly belonging to their Western opponents.

Their victory was as absolute as it was swift and, to the stunned populations of former Imperial Empires in the vast theatre of war, it had come as a revelation. It had been a widespread belief that the Japanese fighting forces were inferior in every respect to the long-established forces of the industrialised defenders. Against the military might and expertise of nations like Great Britain and the United States of America, how could the men of Nippon hope to prevail?

But prevailed they had and not merely through the natural advantage of surprise. It soon became very apparent that the nations waging war in the Pacific in 1941–42 with outdated tactics and obsolete equipment were the Allies and not their despised and underrated opponents.

Pearl Harbor was a clear indication of this fact. Two waves of dive-bombers, torpedo-bombers and fighters had taken off from the decks of six Japanese aircraft-carriers and had, in a few short hours, decimated the main American fleet. The battleships *Arizona*, *California*, *West Virginia* and *Oklahoma* were sunk, the *Nevada*, *Maryland*, *Pennsylvania* and *Tennessee* were all damaged in some degree, three light cruisers were also damaged, as were three destroyers; the mine-layer *Oglala* and the training ship *Utah* were both sunk. In addition over 230 American aircraft were destroyed on the ground and much damage was inflicted on shore installations.

Despite the overwhelming nature of this initial attack however, the Japanese had not become complete masters of the Pacific as, by chance, the American aircraft-carriers had been away from Pearl Harbor at the time. Moreover, in showing the way to the new type of air/sea warfare, the Japanese had let slip the most vital part of the enemy fleet. Although this was over-looked in the general rejoicing, several far-sighted officers fore-saw grim consequences if the US carriers were not sunk soon.

In fact, as one American stated at the time, by sinking and damaging the bulk of the US fleet's battleships the Japanese had, in one stroke, changed the American Navy, 'from a twenty-one knot fleet into a thirty-two knot fleet.'

It could be and indeed it was said that the Pearl Harbor attack proved nothing, in that the American forces were sleeping. The world recognised that although the Americans were well-warned, they were not prepared. But within days, the aircraft of the Japanese Navy were to show, with convincing ease, that they were indeed more than a match for the best the West could produce. In the months which followed, even greater humili-ations were to be heaped upon the Allied nations.

For centuries Great Britain had been the supreme naval power and, under the unchallengeable protection of the Royal Navy, her huge and complex empire had been built up. And although the size of the Royal Navy had been reduced enormously, both in numbers and in equipment since the end of the First World War, it was still numerically the largest fleet in the world and had enormous prestige. Japanese naval officers had been brought up under a system based on the British model and early Japanese ships were designed by British teams. The awe in which the Royal Navy was still held by the native populations of the southeast Asia area should not be underrated. They, like the public at home, considered numbers to be the yardstick for greatness, and could have had no idea just how obsolete and outdated the bulk of the British fleet in 1941 really was. Thus, when the two powerful capital ships, *Prince of Wales* and *Repulse*, arrived to protect Singapore dockyard a great sense of relief prevailed. Alas, this feeling of security was banished within days when both ships were lost in the encounter with the Japanese bombers. Suddenly the whole Malayan peninsula lay open to the invaders.

Nor was this an isolated incident. Hong Kong had fallen and the tentacles of the Japanese octopus were reaching greedily out towards the Philippines, Borneo and the Dutch East Indies, the oil-rich regions which were the main initial objectives of the Japanese advance; for without oil she was a doomed nation.

If the disillusionment of the invincibility of the Royal Navy and the overwhelming strength of the American Navy had both been shattered in a few short hours by a handful of aircraft, then, equally, the military disasters that followed provided the final and complete awakening for the Asiatic subjects of the white master races. 'Impregnable' Singapore surrendered to an army half the size of the defending garrison (the inevitable excuse offered up here was that 'the guns faced the wrong way'). Then, soon after, 'impregnable' Bataan and Corregidor both fell. By this time Borneo had also been lost, the British were evacuating Rangoon in Burma and falling back to the borders of India itself, while Celebes, Timor, Java and Sumatra, of the Dutch East Indies, had also gone under.

To show that the Japanese Navy was as efficient on the surface as it was in the air one only needs to refer to the Battle of the Java Sea which was fought in February 1942. Here a mixed Anglo-American-Dutch squadron of two heavy cruisers, two light cruisers and ten destroyers came up against a Japanese force of two heavy cruisers, two light cruisers and fourteen destroyers. The Japanese were hampered by having a large troop convoy of freighters under its wing. Nevertheless, at the end of the day, the Allied squadron had been completely defeated, losing both the Dutch cruisers and two British destroyers without reply. The surviving Allied warships were then finished off by surface and air attacks during the next few days, only four old American destroyers managing to escape. Java then fell to the Japanese and, shortly afterwards, when a carrier force attacked Port Darwin, sinking twelve ships and causing enormous damage to the harbour installations, the Australians were given a foretaste of things to come.

This was not the end of the story either for, in April, the Japanese sent their fast carrier force westward, into the wide wastes of the Indian Ocean.

Here the British had built up a second fleet in order to defend the sub-continent of India, the oil convoy routes from the Middle East and the flanks of Africa itself. Again, on paper, it was an impressive assembly of warships: five battleships, three aircraft-carriers, two heavy cruisers, five light cruisers and the sixteen destroyers as screen. Impressive it may sound but it must be noted that all the battleships dated back to 1915–16 and only one had been modernised. The three aircraft-carriers were equipped with aircraft that were completely outclassed and outdated (at this stage of the war the Royal Navy was still flying biplanes!), while all the other ships were a very mixed bunch scraped together from many stations with no hope of working together as an efficient fighting team. Commanded by Admiral Somerville, the man who had won fame with Force 'H' in the Mediterranean, it was hoped that this motley collection of vessels could stand up to the six large Japanese carriers. But events proved otherwise and Somerville was completely out-thought by his Japanese opponent Nagumo.

When the Japanese struck at Colombo on 5 April, nineteen of the forty-two British fighters which offered battle were lost as were six torpedo-bombers which arrived at the time of the attack. The Japanese lost only seven aircraft. Meanwhile Somerville had been caught in complete disarray with his fleet dispersed all over the Indian Ocean. Part of it was refuelling at Addu Atoll, one of his aircraft-carriers was at Trincomalee, while two of his heavy cruisers, *Dorsetshire* and *Cornwall*, were both sunk in minutes with no loss whatever to the Japanese force of dive-bombers.

18

A second attack was made by the Japanese carrier force on Trincomalee on the 9th. Here the small British aircraft-carrier *Hermes* was sent out to sea *without any aircraft*! She was located by the Japanese dive-bombers who, delighted at last to have an enemy aircraft-carrier in their grasp, excelled themselves with an example of precision bombing that set the final seal on their six months of operations. The little *Hermes* went down in a deluge of bombs, an estimated forty bombs hitting her in ten minutes! Also sunk were the destroyer *Vampire*, a corvette and two oilers.

On conclusion of this object lesson in the correct use of air/sea power, the Japanese task force sailed back to Japan to refit and refurbish for their next objective, whatever that might be. The Royal Navy hastily withdrew its ancient battleships to East Africa and its Swordfish-equipped carriers likewise kept well away as the long night of Japanese conquest settled down over the former British Empire in Asia. Fortunately the Japanese decided to turn east once more and thus the capitulation of India was avoided. But the loss of face and arms had already sealed the fate of that empire. Not until 1945 was the Royal Navy able to build up sufficient numbers of modern ships and aircraft to return again to the Pacific to offer combat on even equal terms, and by that time much had happened.

To round off their conquests, the so-called 'Far East Co-Prosperity Sphere', the Japanese were determined both to conquer New Guinea and Papua, and to extend their chain of island bases south-eastward, along the Solomons to the New Hebrides and on to Fiji, thus severing the vast continental land mass of Australia from American aid. It could thus be left to wither on the vine.

In pursuing these twin objectives the Japanese sent a troop convoy to Tulagi in April 1942, and started to build an airfield on Guadalcanal, while a second military expedition sailed from their main base at Rabaul, in New Britain, to take Port Moresby on the southern coast of Papua. To cover this operation the Japanese navy drew up two small task forces, one of which was comprised of two aircraft-carriers, two cruisers and six destroyers and was sent into the western part of the Coral Sea, the other, of one small carrier, four cruisers and destroyers, was sent through the Solomon Sea to give the convoy more direct cover.

It was here that the first carrier-to-carrier, air/sea battle took place on 7-9 May, as the Americans had sent a pair of carriers, *Yorktown* and *Lexington*, into the Coral Sea to dispute the invasion. They were escorted by eight cruisers and eleven destroyers.

This first great carrier exchange set the pattern for much of the subsequent naval fighting in the Pacific. It was a confused scramble of air strike and counter strike, of chance, luck and weather often being of more decisive importance than weight of armament, skill or planning. Initially the Americans got in the first blow, sinking the little Japanese carrier *Shoho* on the 7th, maintaining their advantage when the return Japanese strike missed the American carriers but sank an oiler and her destroyer escort instead. The Americans failed to locate the main Japanese carrier force until the next day. Both forces then sent off powerful air strikes and, in the resulting combat, the American aircraft hit, and badly damaged, the large Japanese carrier *Shokaku*, but failed to sink her. The Japanese aircraft in turn hit the *Lexington* and she finally had to be sunk after internal explosions had ripped her apart.

The Battle of the Coral Sea was tactically a draw, with both sides losing a carrier and many aircraft. But the Japanese invasion was frustrated and they decided to attack Port Moresby over land, added to which, their consolidation of the Solomons continued for awhile. While the Americans were naturally jubilant that the hitherto invincible Japanese carriers had at last received a check, the loss of one of their very few carriers was a bad blow, more so since they had news of an even greater operation far to the north.

In relating briefly the Japanese conquests of the opening stages of the Pacific War it is remarkable to note how all this vast area was won, and won decisively, by bold and striking use of very limited forces. In fact the spearhead was the Nagumo strike force and all the other Japanese fleets and armies involved were able to operate with comparative immunity, thanks entirely to the dominance that this remarkably small collection of ships and men had achieved in the Pacific and Indian Oceans.

Not only in this area but in the whole series of wide-ranging operations, the Japanese fought with a limited supply of arms. Their success was even more remarkable due to the fact that they were following a completely opposite strategy to that devised before the war in the event of a conflict with the United States.

When the Washington Treaty of 1921 had frozen the Japanese Navy at sixty per cent of the size of the British and American fleets, Japan had accepted that it would have to fight a defensive war in the Pacific. Power at sea in the '20s and '30s was still estimated by the number of battleships any nation could put into action and, on this score, the Japanese could only total ten against the fifteen of both the Western powers. The strategy devised therefore was for the American fleet to be lured westward, away from their own main bases, into waters of the Japanese Navy's own choosing. There they would be brought to battle and destroyed. The convincing precedent of the destroying of Imperial Russia's Navy in 1904 was obviously the basis for such a policy, combined with their own inferiority of numbers.

The reason for abandoning this theory in favour of all-out attack, was Japan's crucial dependence on imports to keep her going at all. In this she was in exactly the same position of weakness as Great Britain, having to rely on imports to remain alive. But in reality she was in a far greater dilemma than Great Britain, as the latter had the broad Atlantic at her back and a friendly United States to supply her every need, whereas everything vital to Japan's economy lay under the control of her potential enemies. She could not act defensively therefore until she had secured for herself a degree of self-sufficiency, and this meant the conquest of the Dutch East Indies for oil and Malaya for rubber and tin. Both these rich regions were defended by their colonial rulers, and war with the United States therefore meant war with these nations also. How could such a war be contemplated? How could it possibly be undertaken and won from a position of inferiority at sea? There was only one answer and that was by daring, surprise and adoption of a new and revolutionary type of warfare, against which her superior, but more conservative, opponents would have no immediate answer.

Once these initial objectives were taken, then Japan could revert to her old strategy of holding a defensive line in the western Pacific against which the United States would only dash herself in futile assaults until she grew weary of war.

Much of the preparation of Japan's Navy for the waging of such a war depended on the unique use of her air arm, a then untried and suspect part of the overall strength of the navy. The mighty battleships that Japan had in service, together with the even mightier monsters she was building in great secrecy, were to be preserved, held back for the final great deciding battle. What was left then were the aircraft-carriers which were regarded, initially, as expendable anyway, provided they allowed the necessary breathing space for the overall plan to be implemented.

One man, above all others, must stand out in Japanese naval circles as the prophet and wielder of the air arm in its use as the initial striking force of the fleet, and that was Admiral Yamamoto.

The commander-in-chief of the combined fleet, Admiral Isoroku Yamamoto was a man of inspired leadership who was held in complete respect by his subordinates and superiors alike. His judgement on the course of the Pacific War, on the rôle of air power in naval warfare and on the need for Japan to adopt an offensive policy right from the start in order to gain and hold the initiative against a superior combination of opponents, were triumphantly vindicated up until May 1942.

The son of a schoolmaster, he was born in the small village of Kushigun Sonshomura in 1884. His father was fifty-six years old at the time of his birth and thus Yamamoto was named 'Fifty-Six'. At the age of sixteen he entered the Japanese Naval Academy as a cadet. During Japan's coming-of-age war with Russia in 1904–5 Yamamoto served afloat under the great Admiral Togo. In May 1904 during the decisive Battle of Tsushima, Ensign Yamamoto was serving aboard the cruiser *Nisshin*, where he was wounded in action, losing two fingers.

Shortly after getting married he went to Harvard on a two-year course. He was alert and attentive, travelled a great deal and learnt a lot about Americans, their strengths and their weaknesses. He also learnt about the importance of oil and grasped the enormous manufacturing potential of that vast land. He never forgot either.

During the Great War, Japan was a nominal ally of Britain but took little active part in the conflict. Yamamoto however studied all aspects of the war and one facet that fascinated him above all others was the growing power of the aeroplane. The Royal Navy led the world in the development of the aircraft-carrier concept at this time and from a study of their operations, Yamamoto became a firm believer in the future dominance of the aircraft in sea warfare.

In 1923 he was promoted to captain and became executive officer of the air-training centre at Kasumigaura. He learnt to fly and rapidly developed into the leading Japanese theorist on the use of aircraft at sea. With Japan's naval strength frozen by the Washington Naval Treaty to two-thirds of that of Britain or America, Yamamoto began to forecast that this position of inferiority with regard to battleships could be nullified by the correct development of the air arm. This feeling was reinforced by a further term he served as naval attaché in Washington.

His determination that Japan should not become further bound by such treaties was shown in his firm stand taken at the London Naval Conference in 1930. This duty was followed by another period, closer to his heart, as commander of the First Air Fleet. There, he was further able to see that his revolutionary ideas, as they were then, were to some degree carried into force when he was promoted to rear admiral and became head of the technical arm of naval development. Thus, against the wishes of his more conservative fellow officers, he was in a good position to see that Japan's fleet air arm got a fair crack of the whip in any budget expenditure.

At this time Japan's external policy was becoming more openly aggressive. The Manchurian Incident of 1931 being merely the first of several such acts which soon led to all-out war between Japan and China, with her former allies, Great Britain and the United States, becoming increasingly hostile towards her, although powerless to intervene because of their own military weakness and political ineptness.

At the Second London Naval Conference, Yamamoto was again in the forefront, this time as a vice admiral and chief delegate. He travelled to London via the United States and it was at this period that his firm holding out for Japan to have a higher ratio than hitherto allowed was given as the main reason for the failure of the conference to agree on any further limitations.

His reputation for toughness was soon converted by Western newsmen into a fanatical hatred of America, which was just not true. He was however a firm patriot. Under his enthusiastic leadership the development of Japanese naval aviation outstripped that of the West. That the aircraft-carrier would be the dominant weapon of any future Pacific war, Yamamoto remained confident, despite the fact that Japan was also building the largest battleships in the world.

As commander-in-chief on the outbreak of war, his stature was at its peak although he himself, with typical frankness, had no illusions. His oft-quoted statement that Japan could 'run wild' in the first six months of such a war was shown to be true, but so was his prediction that, in the event of the war lasting longer than this period, he had no confidence in Japan's ultimate victory. This was not defeatism but realism. He knew the power of America.

As a man and a leader he was imposing and dominated others equally by his strength of character as by his above-average height. Although a strict disciple of hard training and example, he also had the human failings that endeared him to his junior officers. He was an enthusiastic gambler, he did not drink, but kept a beautiful mistress. He was progressive in his thinking but his devotion to his Emperor was absolute.

One Japanese observer wrote that: 'If, at the start of the Pacific War, a poll had been taken among Japanese naval officers to determine their choice of the man to lead them as Commander-in-Chief Combined Fleet, there is little doubt that Admiral Yamamoto would have been selected by an overwhelming majority.'

Among the Americans at that time, the portrait presented was, understandably enough, rather different. Because of a speech broadcast by Tokyo radio he was widely held to be the arch-villain, threatening to 'dictate a victorious peace in the White House'. He was 'hated and maligned', wrote one historian. When news of his death was brought to Admiral Halsey he is said to have retorted, 'What's good about it? I had hoped to lead that scoundrel up Pennsylvania Avenue in chains . . . '

Before the war however, Yamamoto had not had things all his own way. Initially his new concept of air/sea warfare was as widely derided and opposed among his contemporaries as it was in Britain and America, but Japan was not fettered to the same extent as her western counterparts by reluctant and blind politicians and grasping treasury officials opposed to any arms expenditure. The Japanese government was already set on the road to war and was deeply involved with the conquest of China. They had walked out of the international agreements on arms limitations, and their instructions to the military commanders were merely to build the most formidable weapons they could devise to ensure the superiority of Japanese force of arms in the inevitable ensuing conflict.

Thus, although work commenced on the *Yamato* class battleships, designed to defeat anything then built or being built anywhere in the world, equal importance was given to the development of modern aircraft for the fleet. Nor were these aircraft to be likened to the second-rate conversions and models with which the Royal Navy was saddled at this time. The aircraft that Yamamoto and his team were designing would match the most modern types available to any air force in the world.

Although carrier-aircraft were to be the most vital part of this new air armada, it was acknowledged that the vast areas of the Pacific would necessitate the construction of bombers of the twin-engined type, able to patrol at will over the vital sea routes. Too large for carriers, they were still designed and manned by the Navy for naval operations, and completely attuned to the specialised tasks of naval warfare.

The results of this foresight were invaluable. Firstly there was the Mitsubishi G4M1 Navy Type 1 Land Attack aircraft (code-named 'Betty' by the Allies), a twin-engined aircraft with a crew of six. It had a maximum speed of 354 mph and a range of 3000 miles, and could carry a 1870lb torpedo or two 1100lb bombs. Likewise the Mitsubishi G3M2 'Nell', which was the standard navy bomber on the outbreak of the war. When the ill-fated *Prince of Wales* and *Repulse* sailed on their final voyage their commander had no idea that such aircraft, with such ranges existed, and thought himself comparatively safe from air attack. But that was not the case.

Secondly there was the 'Val' dive-bomber and the 'Kate' torpedo-bomber that formed the basic striking units for the carriers of the Imperial Japanese Navy. Both proved to be deadly in their accuracy and efficiency while continued training had brought their crews to perfection, as was demonstrated time and time again. It was this combination of dive- and torpedo-bombers that was to drive the battleship ultimately from the sea. By contrast, high-level bombing of warships at sea, as championed by the Royal Air Force and the USAAF at that time, proved the ultimate in futility, and *no* major warship was ever sunk at sea by such a method, despite innumerable claims to the contrary.

Finally, to win dominance over the battleground wherever it was, the Japanese flyers of the Imperial Navy had the 'Zero' or 'Zeke' fighter, an aircraft which completely outclassed any other aircraft in the Pacific in 1941–42. A single-seater inter-ceptor designed specifically for carrier work and therefore having sturdiness and range, combined with speed and power, this aircraft ensured that, when the Japanese went to war, com-plete air domination was theirs from the start.

The Japanese carrier fleet had been steadily built up in the pre-war years from lowly beginnings. The first fully fledged carrier to be built was the little *Hosho* in 1922. Although only 7500 tons and able to carry only twenty-one aircraft at 25 knots, she performed valuable training duties. From this embryo the Japanese went for much larger vessels with the *Kaga* (38,200 tons, 90 aircraft, 28 knots), and the *Akagi* (36,500 tons, 91 air-craft, 31 knots), both converted from large battleships and battle-cruisers built in the '20s. Both these ships were part of the Nagumo strike force. Two more carriers joined the fleet in the late 1930s, these were the sister ships *Hiryu* and *Soryu* (15,900 tons, 73 aircraft, 34 knots). Of more moderate tonnage, they nevertheless carried a good complement of aircraft and were fast. They were followed by another two large vessels, *Shokaku* and *Zuikaku* (25,670 tons, 84 aircraft, 34 knots), which combined the best features of the preceding classes.

With the rapid expansion of the naval air arm the need was for more carriers to be built rapidly and so several smaller ships were again built to join the older *Ryujo* (10,600 tons, 48 aircraft, 29 knots). This was achieved by converting fast tankers and liners into medium-sized carriers and in this way the *Shoho* and *Zuiho* (11,260 tons, 30 aircraft, 28 knots), *Chuyo*, *Taiyo* and *Unyo* (17,830 tons, 27 aircraft, 21 knots), and *Hiyo* and *Junyo* (24,100 tons, 53 aircraft, 25 knots), all joined the fleet between 1941 and late 1942.

In numbers the air arm of the Japanese Navy stood at some 500 carrier-based fighters, 200 dive-bombers, 430 torpedo-bombers, plus 370 land-based bombers for front-line duties. Thus the pre-war statements by American magazines that, ' . . . the Japanese navy air force consists of four aircraft-carriers and 200 planes . . . ' were just so much 'informed' nonsense.

To back up this carrier force was an equally formidable Japanese surface fleet. Apart from the ten battleships built, and the others being built, there was a fine force of modern heavy cruisers, fast and heavily armed with 8in guns, scores of the big new destroyers, the most advanced ships of this type in the world with dual-purpose guns in turrets and the incredible 'Long Lance' torpedo that outranged anything in the Allies' arsenals, and a large submarine fleet. Furthermore it was a fleet manned by highly trained and confident men, an élite force in every sense. This was its great strength against the hotch-potch forces ranged against them. However, it was ultimately its greatest weakness. For the veterans who went to war in December 1941 were gradually to be whittled down and never replaced. Nor could the industrial potential of Japan ever hope to match the power of the United States. In material, if the Americans were found to be weaker at the start of the war, they had the industrial strength, and technological know-how, to out-build Japan many times over. The Japanese knew this, and realised that they must wage a lightning war and then hold firm their outer perimeter of defences.

Ironic though it may seem, it was their very success that unhinged this sound war-plan. The great conquests had been made so quickly and so cheaply that it led them to try for even greater prizes in the belief that they were invincible. This is certainly understandable when one pictures the actual rate of loss during the first six months of the war. Japan had gained an enormous empire and her losses in warships, despite incredible claims to the contrary by American and British press and radio sources, had been minimal. In all, the Japanese had lost the small carrier *Shoho*, one seaplane tender, one mine-layer and six destroyers. By contrast the Allied powers had lost, in the same period of time, the carriers *Lexington* and *Hermes*, nine battleships, a seaplane tender, four heavy cruisers, three light cruisers and seventeen destroyers.

Although the American carriers had been spared from the disaster at Pearl Harbor, they had not yet made their presence felt to any large degree, until the Coral Sea battle. This continued to trouble the Japanese high command who, despite their string of easy victories, kept looking over their shoulders into the wide expanse of the broad Pacific and wondering just when and where the expected counter-attack would come.

So far things had gone perfectly and, now that the initial objectives had been secured, the second part of the plan could be put into effect. The remaining strength of the American fleet, which was in fact all that stood between Japan and total victory, had to be lured out to combat and finally and completely destroyed. How best to carry out this final reckoning was what troubled them, for now a new facet had made the old 'wait-and-see' policy too passive.

This new facet was the launching from the flight deck of an American carrier of a squadron of twin-engined Mitchell bombers (B-25s) for a daring raid on Tokyo and other Japanese cities. The damaged inflicted by this raid was minimal, the merest pin-prick, and it was doubtful whether it could ever have been repeated. But the moral damage, the loss of face, the sheer shock of seeing even a solitary American bomber over the home islands when the Japanese had felt themselves invulnerable behind their new perimeters of conquest, contributed

28

to the various arguments that were going on about future strategy. Japanese dignity could not allow such a shameful thing to happen again.

So the Doolittle raid had an effect out of all proportion and, instead of being just a propaganda point for the victory-starved American public to be pap-fed on to take their minds off greater disasters, it proved to be a major contribution to what was to be the most decisive naval battle in the history of Japan and the United States.

It will be convenient here to examine the conflicting plans put forward to bring the war to a successful conclusion, now that Japan had achieved her aim of self-sufficiency.

After Malaya and Burma had fallen, plans for the conquest of Ceylon were given consideration. However they were abandoned when the army refused to allocate the necessary divisions for such an operation. Their eyes were firmly fixed on Russia and they wished to retain the bulk of their ground forces to exploit the expected Soviet collapse after the German offensive of 1942. With no aid to be expected from the army, save in small detachments, the plan to drive south-east and isolate Australia continued to be pressed forward, even after the slight set-back of the Coral Sea battle. Thus, although already committed to one line of advance, the Japanese now considered a second and third front in the Pacific.

In order to lure the American fleet to its doom the occupation of the Hawaiian islands was suggested. Not only would this eliminate the only remaining naval base the Americans had in the Pacific, but it would certainly ensure that they sent every available ship and plane out in its defence. However it was agreed that Hawaii would be a tough nut to crack and an alternative target which might have the same effect at less initial risk was sought. Once the American fleet was destroyed, Hawaii would fall anyway.

After the brilliant success of the Pearl Harbor attack, of which he was the main driving force, Admiral Yamamoto's prestige was at its peak. All planning was under his authority and he was convinced that the destruction of the American fleet overrode every other consideration. He instructed his chief of staff's planning officer, Commander Yasuji Watanabe, to work out the details of a plan that he had nurtured for years, the invasion of Midway – Plan 'AF'.

This plan was not however favourably received by the Naval General Staff and Yamamoto had to fight hard to convince his fellow officers that it was the only course to take. His toughest fight proved to be with Commander Miyo of naval operations, though he did succeed fairly quickly in winning over Admiral Nagumo of the carrier strike force, who was initially opposed to it. Nagumo was later to be of great importance in the overall plan.

The original choice of Vice Admiral Chuichi Nagumo to the command of the First Air Fleet, Japan's most powerful instrument of war, had been at first sight a strange one. Nagumo was by no means closely identified with the pro-air faction of the Imperial Navy and knew little or nothing of flying operations and tactics.

He was, in fact, a traditional officer of the old school, and his speciality was in the torpedo field, in which he was acknowledged as an expert. His previous experience in the fleet had been of a routine nature and since his early days he had spent a great part of his time ashore. He had served as part of the Naval General Staff and at the Navy Ministry in largely administrative rôles and had been an instructor at the Naval War College.

The choice of Nagumo probably rested on his known determination to ensure that Japan's navy should be second to none in size and power. He took a prominent part in organising resistance to the Washington Naval Treaty in the fleet and gained the sympathies of the more aggressive younger officers in this way. Certainly in time of war his qualities as an aggressive officer were a prime requirement in his later task of commanding the fleet's spearhead.

Afloat he had served as captain of the crusier *Takao* in the early 1930s. She was part of cruiser division 4 of the second fleet, which was the advance force of the combined fleet. Here his special knowledge of torpedo operations fully suited his position and he was a calm, confident figure, sure of his job. The same applied, with even more emphasis, when he was a rear admiral with destroyer squadron 1. The big new destroyers of this force regarded themselves, quite rightly, as a specialist élite. The rôle of the destroyer in Japan's naval history led them to acquire a special kudos for daring, bravery and skill. Moreover the Japanese destroyers of this period led the world by at least a decade in design and fighting power.

It was principally a torpedo striking force and the Japanese ships carried very powerful outfits of the new 'Long Lance' torpedo, a weapon which exceeded any similar weapon in any other fleet's armoury in range and destructive power. It was expected to be a decisive influence in any fleet engagement in the old-style surface-to-surface combats still envisaged as the setpiece battle *par excellence* as laid down in the Japanese war plan.

Here Nagumo's influence could be put to perfect use, and the very high degree of skill and expertise developed by the Japanese destroyer forces, which were to be ably demonstrated in the Pacific War in the coming months, owe a great deal to his guidance in night-fighting and torpedo tactics.

But despite his skill in these fields, as commander of the First Air Fleet Nagumo was very much a fish out of water. Because of this, his handling of the carriers was marked throughout by a great deal of caution and hesitancy.

It might seem strange to state that the victor of such smashing surprise victories as Pearl Harbor and the Indian Ocean foray should have been cautious, but, on close examination, it can be substantiated.

Nagumo was bitterly criticised by many Japanese flyers for not sending in a second attack against Pearl Harbor when the American defences were smashed flat but the operating facilities of the base itself were still largely intact. In a similar manner, although he achieved much in the Indian Ocean, and sent the British fleet scuttling back to Africa, he showed a similar reluctance to close his enemy. This failure to get to grips firmly with his opponents while he still had overwhelming power, in both cases ultimately enabled them to get back on their feet again for the counter-attack.

The fact that he was so severely taken to task for this Pearl Harbor episode probably weighed heavily in the balance during

31

the Midway operation when, at a similar critical moment, he was faced with an identical problem: whether to attack a second time, or to withdraw and hold himself ready for a counter-blow.

As a man he inspired confidence in his men by his devotion to his work and his logical approach to difficult problems. He had a warm personality and was popular. Six months of high-pressure warfare had left its mark on him by May 1942. He was tired, he was out of his depth with air fighting and he had a natural concern of any good commanding officer for his men, who, he was well aware, shared his weariness. As a result he was not in top form for the coming battle, a battle that was to be far more taxing and demanding than any of his easy conquests to date.

Thus it can be seen that although Nagumo accepted Yamamoto's plans, he did so with reservations. This was not the case with Commander Miyo.

Miyo held, with some considerable sense, that the occupation of Midway would not in any way help Japan's war effort. It was, he pointed out, only 1100 miles away from Pearl Harbor and, even if occupied, could never be held by the Japanese; the lines of communication would be too long for that. Nor was he convinced, even if it could be somehow held and utilised without disturbance, whether it would serve any useful purpose, isolated as it was. The theory that search planes from the island base would act as an early-warning station to prevent a repetition of the Doolittle raid he held to be worthless, for the island could be by-passed with ease. It would merely be a liability.

Further than this however, he felt that, in estimating that the Americans would fight with every ship they possessed for this insignificant scrap of sand and coral, Yamamoto and his supporters were merely indulging in wishful thinking. Miyo much preferred the original plan of attack, through Fiji and Samoa. Here he felt the cutting off of Australia was much more likely to bring about the hoped-for decisive battle, for America could not abandon her one remaining ally in the Pacific theatre.

The discussions dragged on and then went further up the chain to Admiral Ito, Deputy Chief of Naval Staff, and Commander Miyo also convinced Rear Admiral Fukudome, the

32

head of operations, that Yamamoto's plan was impracticable. Yamamoto however remained absolutely adamant, his was the *only* plan which he could foresee would bring the final victorious naval action they all knew was essential. Faced with such stubbornness and inflexibility by the most respected of their naval commanders, and one, moreover, who had been so recently and triumphantly vindicated by events, the opposition gave way. Plan AF was approved.

Events were to prove Admiral Yamamoto's reasoning correct, for the Americans were determined to react vigorously against any thrust against Midway Island.

'Midway Island acts as a sentry for Hawaii,' Admiral Nagumo had stated and the Americans were keenly aware of the fact.

Even though the naval staff had given their reluctant approval to Plan AF, Yamamoto's struggles continued, for neither Vice Admiral Kondo, nor Admiral Nagumo at first, knew of the plan and the commander of the Fourth Fleet, Vice Admiral Inouye, stated plainly that he had absolutely no confidence in the plan at all. It was the Doolittle raid that put a final end to this bickering, and although many still held reservations, Plan AF was embraced by the commanders of the various Japanese fleets. The army, too, offered no objections, primarily because the limited type of occupation envisaged would place no great demands on them or their resources.

The basic plan then was a sound one, and one that showed every sign of success. If Midway was occupied, so much the better, but this was not absolutely essential. What was essential was that America would come to the aid of the tiny garrison. It therefore behove the Japanese to be on hand with every available ship and plane to ensure that this sought-after battle, if it took place, could only result in a Japanese victory. But it was at this point that over-confidence began to cloud the hitherto impeccable judgement of the naval planners.

Considering that the objective of their assault was twice as far from Japanese bases as from Hawaii, it was absolutely essential to the Japanese plan that everything should be totally concentrated on this one operation. But it was not, for the completely unnecessary complication of the occupation of islands in the mist-shrouded Aleutians, in the north Pacific, was tacked on to the Midway plan. The allocation of two light carriers to this operation straightaway made nonsense of the old dictum of concentration at the main point of battle.

Secondly there was the haste in which the operation was pressed forward from the moment final approval was received. In war it is certainly desirable to be 'the firstest with the mostest', but not at the expense of detailed planning. Such was the vast scope and size of the operation, that time in which the various fleet commanders could discuss the battle plan, was at a premium. Furthermore, the steel tip of the whole Japanese plan was once again to be the six carriers (reduced to four after Coral Sea) of the redoubtable Nagumo force. But, as we have seen, the aircrew and ships' companies of this élite group had just returned from the Indian Ocean after completing a six-month tour of operations conducted at an unprecedented pitch. Both the men and the machines needed time for resting and refitting before embarking on the greatest test of their skills yet to arise: direct combat with the American carriers. They were not to get that time.

Final preparations now went ahead at an accelerated pace for Plan AF. Virtually the whole combat strength of the Japanese Navy was to be committed to the operation and it was thought that, at the crucial time, Yamamoto's force would enjoy such overwhelming superiority as to make victory a certainty.

The actual plan itself was rehearsed in an elaborate war game and the results were confirmed as an overwhelming victory for the Japanese forces, with every objective attained at minimal loss. However, this result was hardly objective, the Japanese umpires' decisions being overruled by Rear Admiral Ugaki, thus making the whole conclusion a farce. For example the umpires ruled that during a mock attack on Midway, shore-based aircraft struck the Nagumo force and both *Akagi* and *Kaga* were sunk. However the judges were overruled and both ships took part in subsequent parts of the game. On being closely examined as to what allowance had been made should an enemy carrier group appear on their flanks while their own aircraft were attacking Midway no clear answer was forthcoming – a highly unsatisfactory state of affairs.

Moreover air combat training, carried out at this time for the replacement aircrews, revealed that their skills were far below that of the veteran flyers already with the fleet. An early and startling warning as to just how much the Japanese depended on a select élite rather than on a broad-based force.

It was thought that the Americans had no battleships available for combat in the central Pacific at this time, but, even should they assemble a squadron, Japan's battleship strength was intact and Admiral Yamamoto would be flying his flag in the *Yamato*, the first of the super-giants to join the fleet. With her nine 18in guns, the largest calibre to be taken to sea by any navy, and backed by the rest of the front-line battle fleet, Yamamoto could be confident in facing any surface threat that the Americans might offer.

In the air he was equally confident, in fact over-confident. It was estimated that the total number of carriers the Americans could deploy against his force was three, whereas a total of six were with the Midway force, with a further two to be assigned to the Aleutians. In fact the Japanese should, and could, have deployed a further two, for, although both *Shokaku* and *Zuikaku* had been damaged at Coral Sea, neither of them was written off. They could easily have been got ready but Yamamoto was confident that a two-to-one margin was sufficient; another example of over-confidence. *Zuikaku* in fact was in a fit enough state to sail, but lacked trained aircrew due to losses. The transfer of the survivors of the *Shokaku*'s air group to make up the deficiency was rejected and she remained at home.

In other classes of warship, the Japanese were equally well placed. In total they planned to utilise no less than twenty-four cruisers and seventy destroyers, while fifteen submarines were deployed to the east of Midway to lie in wait for the American fleet should it venture forth. It was thought that the Americans could deploy only nine cruisers and thirty destroyers against this force, plus about twenty-five submarines. In actual fact in all classes, save for submarines, the Americans had *fewer* vessels than the Japanese allowed for.

The actual landing force was composed of the troops of Colonel Kiyonao Ichiki's Midway landing force: 1500 marines as assault troops for Sand Island itself, 1000 soldiers to take Eastern Island, these being the two principal islands of the atoll, and two construction battalions, whose task would be to put the islands back into a state of defence against the expected American counter-attacks. In all, some 5000 men were embarked in the fifteen transports, under the overall command of Captain Minoru Ota (the navy's marine unit, the 'Kure' special naval landing force, being a larger group than Colonel Ichiki's detachment).

This transport group was escorted by destroyer squadron 2, under the command of Rear Admiral Tanaka, with one light cruiser, ten destroyers, and an oiler. Also sailing in company with this group was the seaplane tender group commanded by Rear Admiral Fujita. The task of this force was to occupy Kure Island and set up a seaplane base there in conjunction with the main operation. For this subsidiary operation the seaplane tenders had a solitary destroyer escort which was not expected to be opposed. A special minesweeper group, under the command of Captain Miyamoto, was also to proceed to the assembly point via Wake Island. This comprised three supply ships, four minesweepers and three small subchasers.

To provide heavy support for these slow and vulnerable groups, Vice Admiral Kondo would be guarding their southern flank with the invasion force main body, comprising the fast battleships *Hiei* and *Kongo*, the light carrier *Zuiho*, four heavy and one light cruiser and eight destroyers. Nearer in would be the close support group of Vice Admiral Kurita, with four heavy cruisers and two destroyers.

All these groups were collectively known as the Midway invasion force and their tasks were itemised as follows.

N-Day (as the Japanese termed the actual landing day, the equivalent to the Allied D-Day, but only for this operation) was set to be 7 June 1942. On N-minus 1 (6 June) the crews of the seaplane tenders were to walk ashore at Kure Island, some sixty miles north-west of Midway and establish a reconnaissance base to act in conjunction with the main fleets.

At dawn on N-Day the marines and the Ichiki detachment

36

were to storm ashore on Sand and Eastern Islands and direct heavy gunfire support would be provided by the heavy cruisers of Rear Admiral Kurita. Kondo would keep to the south or south-west with his heavy units, ready to intervene if called upon and to provide a fast and powerful heavy reserve for the expected main fleet action.

On completion of the occupation, the atoll was to be put into a state of defence, but later the army units would be withdrawn and replaced by naval units, so that the ultimate defence of the atoll would be exclusively a naval matter.

This was only the landing side of the story however. Before this could take place the Midway defences would have to be pulverised by massive air attacks launched from the Nagumo carriers. These were planned to take place on N-minus 2 (5 June).

However, as we have seen, the occupation of Midway was of secondary importance to bringing the Americans to battle. To this end the main units of the Japanese Navy were deployed.

The focal point of these forces, and of the battle, was the Nagumo force, now reduced as we noted, to four carriers, *Akagi*, *Kaga*, *Hiryu* and *Soryu*, with a total of eighty-four fighters, eighty-four dive-bombers and ninety-three torpedo-bombers embarked. Heavy gun support for the carriers was provided as usual by the battleships *Haruna* and *Kirishima*, two heavy and one light cruiser and the eleven destroyers of destroyer squadron 10. On N-minus 2, they would launch an air strike against Midway Island itself from a position some two hundred and fifty miles to the north-west of the atoll which would destroy American aircraft and shore installations and any shipping found in the vicinity. A second strike would go in, if it was thought necessary, and then the force would move to its waiting position to meet the American fleet.

It will not pass unnoticed that the Japanese plans envisaged their achieving complete surprise. No reaction was expected from the main US fleet until *after* the initial assaults had taken place and Midway had been occupied. With this belief, the movements of the expected main fleet action were synchronised to take place during the period N-plus 1 to N-plus 7 – by that time the supporting forces should all have been up in support of the carriers.

The ultimate decision on the selected field of battle would then be decided by the fire-power of the battleships of the main body commanded by Admiral Yamamoto himself. This force comprised the battleships *Yamato*, *Nagato* and *Mutsu*, which had the small carrier *Hosho* as air defence and were screened by the light cruiser *Sendai* and nine destroyers. Also attached to this force were the seaplane tenders *Chiyoda* and *Nisshin*. Sailing as part of this group were the battleships *Hyuga*, *Ise*, *Fuso* and *Yamashiro* under command of Vice Admiral Takasu. Known as the guard force they were to deploy separately to provide heavy cover for the Aleutians operation. These four battleships were screened by the light cruisers *Oi* and *Kitakami* and twelve destroyers. These seven battleships, plus the two with Nagumo and the two with Kondo, gave the Japanese an overwhelmingly heavy fire-power base. Unfortunately, instead of concentrating his eleven mighty battleships close to his carriers, Yamamoto had split them up, as he had his carriers, and diversified their fire-power, leaving them well in the back field where they could not use their huge guns to any effect.

To set up advance submarine cordon lines by N-minus 5 the Japanese also deployed a large submarine force under the overall command of Vice Admiral Komatsu in his cruiser flagship *Katori* at Kwajalein. Cordon A consisted of the five submarines of squadron 3 which were placed between Midway and the approaches from Hawaii, south of French Frigate Shoals, in a north-south line. North of this position a second line was established by the seven boats of squadron 5, known as cordon B. They deployed in a line roughly south-east to north-west. Between them these submarines should have been able to guard shipping routes coming directly up from Pearl Harbor.

However, to provide similar warning against the approach of the US fleet swinging into the north of Midway, a third cordon C, was established, again running north-south with three boats of squadron 1.

In addition to these forces, the shore-based air force of Vice Admiral Tsukahara was also to co-operate in the assault by redeploying from the nearest island bases to Midway and by providing the aircraft to be based at the atoll once under Japanese control. For these rôles, Tsukahara had thirty-six fighters embarked in the carriers, ten bombers, based on Wake Island and six long-range flying boats, based at Jaluit. He was supported by the 24th Air Flotilla under Rear Admiral Maeda with three separate air groups totalling seventy-two fighters, seventy-two torpedo-bombers and eighteen flying boats..

The fighters and torpedo aircraft were based at Wake, Wotje, Aur and Kwajalein while the flying boats moved into Jaluit and Wotje. However, from the nearest Japanese base, Wotje, to Hawaii was 2000 miles and, in order to extend their reconnaissance capabilities to cover this huge gap, special long-range Kawanishi 2 flying boats with 4000 mile range were to be utilised, using a secret anchorage at French Frigate Shoals as a refuelling base, and taking on fuel from submarines waiting there for them. Known as operation 'K', this daring plan called for two of the big flying boats to conduct a last-minute reconnaissance flight over Oahu itself.

The Aleutian Islands plan was an afterthought and it has no place in our story, other than to record that it utilised two carriers, three heavy cruisers, three light cruisers, twelve destroyers, forty fighters, twenty-one dive-bombers and twenty-one torpedo-bombers that would have proved invaluable at Midway itself. Also, it further complicated the Midway plan by requiring its own submarine patrol line and the dividing of the main battleship force as already recorded. It took place successfully, but the capture of the islands of Attu and Kiska was a pyrrhic victory and proved of absolutely no value to the Japanese, other than as a useful propaganda exercise.

Having lightly sketched in the Japanese objectives and plans, together with their initial dispositions it might be a good place for the reader to refer to the full list of the actual fighting strength of this enormous armada on the eve of battle contained in *Appendix One* (page 175).

Never had such a fleet sailed with such overwhelming confidence, and justified confidence in the light of its recent achievements, as did Yamamoto's command. Never before had the odds been so much on one side in sheer weight of numbers, expertise and fire-power. It was a fleet to marvel at. Little wonder then, when the Japanese admiral surveyed his vast command, that he sailed forth to the east without hesitation and sure of complete victory, convinced that his plan was perfect.

But as we have seen, his plan was not perfect. Although he had all the ships and aircraft he had called for, his chain of command was a complicated one. The breaking up of his valuable forces into groups and sub-groups, each separated from the other by hundreds of miles of water so that they could not quickly concentrate to aid each other, seems strange. But in the battle as he planned it, all these diverging forces would confuse the enemy. The Americans would not know where to strike first, they would be surrounded on all sides and then annihilated.

Nothing had been left to chance. Nothing, save for the fact that the Americans might just possibly have plans of their own!

CHAPTER TWO

THE NUT

In the months that had followed Pearl Harbor the United States
Navy had been on the defensive everywhere. But it was not a
rôle that came naturally to it. Ever since the end of the Great
War, American naval thought had been directed to one end,
the creation of 'a Navy second-to-none', and, although the
various disarmament conferences and the stringent economic
climate of the '20s and '30s had seen the continued restrictions
of this policy, by the early 1940s they were in sight of their goal.

America had been steadily building up her strength at sea
since the 1890s but it was the aftermath of the Great War, which
left the hitherto unassailable European sea powers both
exhausted and war-weary, and, more to the point, almost bank-
rupt, which had given her her chance to reach parity with Great
Britain, long acknowledged *the* sea power. And this had been
done more by diplomatic means than by a heavy ship-building
programme. In 1919 Great Britain had sixty-three battleships
and America a mere twenty. By 1922 both powers were equal.
But this was not all, for during the two decades of peace, the
United States had evaluated the concepts of future requirements
much more accurately than had Britain. Unshackled by inter-
departmental control over her naval aviation, America had
made great strides in this field and her aircraft and carriers were
among the best-equipped in the world. Moreover she had
developed a number of air-minded admirals over this period
and this forward-looking policy, when coupled to her un-
matched industrial capacity, meant that she was able to outbuild
any of her rivals with ease once the go-ahead was given. This
happened with the plan to create a 'Two-Ocean Navy' and when
this vast building programme, undertaken in 1940, was complete

America would have been unassailable at sea. However, in the bleak months of early 1942, most of the new ships of that programme were still on the stocks and America had to fight across the wastes of the Pacific only with what ships she had available.

The great fortune that preserved her aircraft-carriers when her battlefleet was lost necessitated the swing to carrier-based warfare, but this had already been studied at great length before the war. Even so the power of their opponents had meant that the carriers available to the Pacific fleet had been able to do little more than stage pin-prick raids on outlying Japanese bases. At home the public became restive with apparent lack of action, but only the commanders on the spot realised what a pitiful shoe-string they were fighting the war on.

Several of the old battleships had survived the Pearl Harbor attack, and others were transferred from the Atlantic, but these could not hope to match the Japanese in gun power now.

Nor were these old battleships fast enough to indulge in the hit-and-run-type attacks now taking place, and were withdrawn to the west coast of America to refurbish and re-equip. New, fast battleships were being completed but, until they could take their place in line, only heavy cruisers could accompany the carriers on their missions. Obviously the Americans had to rely on 'stand-off' tactics in the interim.

All then rested on the carriers, but here also the Americans were vastly outclassed at this time. *Lexington* had been lost at Coral Sea, *Saratoga* had just completed repairs after being hit by a submarine torpedo earlier in the war, and her new air group was not yet combat-ready. The *Wasp* had been in the European theatre of war and was still in the Atlantic and *Yorktown* had been very badly damaged at Coral Sea. This left just the *Enterprise* and *Hornet* to hold the ring against all that the enemy could throw. The Japanese also had the initiative. Over the whole vast Pacific how and when they would strike next was unknown to the Americans. They only knew that two carriers could not hope to cover the whole potential front.

Away across the Indian Ocean the Royal Navy had two brand-new carriers with armoured decks, *Illustrious* and *Indomitable*, with a third, *Victorious*, on the way. An urgent appeal for help was made to the Admiralty to send at least one of these ships to help in the coming battle, but the reply received was that 'none could be spared'. True, with their obsolete aircraft, they would have been of little help, and the time taken for the ships to sail the 11,000 miles from East Africa to Pearl Harbor would have made them too late anyway. The Americans now knew they were on their own.

In one respect however the United States naval commanders were ahead of the game. They *knew* exactly where and when the next Japanese attack was coming!

The work of Commander Joseph J. Rochefort Jr and his team of intelligence officers and cryptanalysts of the navy combat intelligence unit at Pearl Harbor played an outstanding part in this vital battle. During April and May they steadily analysed the streams of information coming over the intercepted airwaves. It was obvious that something very big was brewing. The vital questions of course were where and when.

Admiral Chester W. Nimitz, commander-in-chief of the Pacific fleet, began to receive a steady flow of reports based on this intercepted traffic and on the educated guesses of 'black chamber' staff at Pearl, which indicated that the offensive was coming in May and that it would be aimed straight down his throat . . . at Midway, as a stepping stone to Hawaii.

Although the evidence was at first fragmentary, it kept piling up. Constant references in Japanese codes to Plan AF were studied. It was apparent after a short while that AF was the big one and by 14 May Nimitz was convinced enough of his hunches to order a state of 'fleet opposed invasion' for the Hawaii area. In Washington Admiral Ernest King and his staff had reached the same conclusions and he predicted from his intelligence sources that the end of May would see an expeditionary force sailing to seize Midway. There was still some opinion in American circles that the more likely target of such a massive attack would be Oahu itself but, whichever the target, it was clear that a major clash was but a matter of weeks away. How would they meet it and with what?

To test their predictions Rochefort suggested the planting of false information about Midway's defences to see if there was any reaction. An uncoded radio signal was sent from the atoll, stating that its distillation plant had broken down. Careful watch on the suspected Japanese frequencies was rewarded when they picked up a signal confirming to the AF planners that Midway would be short of water!

Nimitz had already estimated that in sheer numbers and hardware he would be heavily outnumbered so that when it was realised that the planned operation was to be a dual one, with the occupation of the Aleutians taking place at the same time, he had no hesitation in deciding to ignore this northern threat as a diversion he could not cover. Everything he had must be concentrated around Midway. In truth there was very little.

As well as the remarkable success of the intelligence unit in so accurately predicting the target of the Japanese offensive and the timing of the attack down to the days of sailing for the various forces involved, Nimitz had one more thing working for him at this time. This was the efficiency of the dockyard at Pearl Harbor, coupled with the desire of every commander under his control to face the enemy once and for all. The time of retreat and side-stepping was over and the spirit of the fleet was high.

This determination was reflected in the story of the *Yorktown*.

After the severe hammering she had taken in the Coral Sea battle, when a heavy bomb had disembowelled her and several near misses had caused her to leak like a colander, careful estimates put the time required to make good her damage and get her patched up ready for combat again at ninety days.

On 27 May *Yorktown* limped into Pearl Harbor and went straight into dry-dock. Every man available, some 1400 in all, went quickly and smoothly into action. Working in shifts day and night, ignoring blueprints and working flat out against the clock the yard performed a miracle. Not ninety days but two passed and on 29 May the dock was flooded and the *Yorktown* floated out. With workmen still aboard, steam was raised, refuelling completed and on 30 May she put to sea after embarking a hastily assembled air group made up from three different carriers. It was a repair job that no other nation could have done, or even attempted. The contrast to this all-out effort by the Americans and the indifferent handling of the *Shokaku* and *Zuikaku* is marked. The Japanese were convinced they had more than enough ships for the coming battle, the Americans knew

44

they were going to need every last one. As a result three big American carriers now faced four big Japanese ones. The odds, in the air anyway, were levelling up and, when one counts the actual number of combat aircraft embarked, one sees how the scales had begun to tilt even more back towards the Americans in this field: 233 American against 272 Japanese.

In addition to the three carriers and their air groups, on which the main brunt of the battle naturally fell, it was hoped that some shore-based support from Midway atoll itself might further help redress the balance.

The *Enterprise* and *Hornet* were the core of the newly formed task force 16 which had just returned from the south Pacific after a futile attempt to intervene in the Coral Sea battle. This task force had the two-fisted Hustlin' Halsey, Vice Admiral W. F. Halsey, as its commander, but a skin disease had incapacitated him at this vital time and when the group returned to Pearl for refuelling on 26 May, he was relieved in command by Rear Admiral Raymond Ames Spruance, hitherto in command of the heavy cruiser squadrons. He had a reputation for unflappability, a quality that was to be much tested in the coming battle.

When Admiral Halsey selected Spruance to take over his staff aboard *Enterprise* it was an inspired judgement, although a man more unlike Halsey it would be hard to imagine than Spruance.

Like Nagumo on the Japanese side, Spruance was not a 'carrier man' at all, although as commander of cruiser division 5 of Halsey's task force, he was given ample and detailed opportunity to absorb the many initial lessons of carrier combat in the live conditions of war.

Born in 1887, he, like Nagumo, had spent a large proportion of his service in staff capacities. He had graduated from Annapolis in 1906 and had spent a period at the Naval War College. He made his mark in the naval intelligence field and again returned to the War College at Rhode Island for two periods in the 1930s.

It was probably this grounding that developed his ability to carefully and diligently study each problem that came up. He was an abstainer from drink and tobacco and had an intense dislike for publicity, in direct contrast to his predecessor. Quiet and thoughtful, he was a great walker. His intenseness and methodical approach to every situation earned him a reputation of aloofness.

From 1938 he had commanded the battleship *Mississippi* and, on promotion to rear admiral, he had been placed in command of cruiser division 5. With this force of heavy cruisers he had provided the only 'heavy' fire-power the United States Navy had left in the Pacific Ocean for the first months of 1942. They gave their protection to the *Enterprise* and *Hornet* on their various sorties in the vastness of the Japanese-dominated wastes as Halsey conducted his daring raids.

In February Halsey had attacked the Marshalls and soon afterwards his bombers hit Marcus Island while Fletcher in *Yorktown* struck at the Gilberts. The cruisers carried out bombardments and, although the targets were sparse to say the least, they were successful.

In between these excursions they bombarded Wake Island on 24 February, beating off a light air raid. Of course these raids were mere pin-pricks, and as one of the war correspondents aboard one of Spruance's ships recorded:

'You steam about ten thousand miles, you fire twenty-five rounds a gun. You go away leaving land batteries and ground installations and power plants and God knows what. And if those bombs had hit us an hour ago, you could rate this as a very expensive expedition . . . '

But they were learning. The next operation that Spruance's cruisers escorted was the Doolittle raid. Again actual damage inflicted was negligible but it gave US morale a boost at a bad time and it gave Spruance and others invaluable experience in operating over huge areas of ocean and refuelling at sea.

If Spruance was not a carrier expert he knew enough of the ropes by now to take command. With his enormous tactical expertise and with Halsey's experienced staff to help him, it was not such an overwhelming responsibility. And in the event Rear Admiral Spruance was to prove himself the complete master of the situation, reading the course of the battle with unrivalled clarity. He went on to become one of the most successful carrier admirals of the whole Pacific war. His master stroke being the battle of the Philippine Sea, or 'Great Marianas

Turkey Shoot' when his similar careful tactics resulted in the destruction of ninety per cent of the Japanese aircraft taking part. But that was in the future; at this point in time Admiral Spruance had just one week for the preparation of himself, and his team, to face the supreme test of a new commander: all-out battle.

For 'heavy metal' Spruance could only call on the heavy cruisers of Rear Admiral Kinkaid's squadron of five ships, while a slender destroyer screen of nine ships was assembled. Two oilers with a two-destroyer escort were also assigned to the group.

Task force 17 was built around the freshly repaired *Yorktown* and placed under the command of Rear Admiral Jack Fletcher, once more eager to avenge the loss of the *Lexington* the month before.

Frank Fletcher, with the recent experience of the Coral Sea battle still fresh in his mind, was probably the most experienced of the American carrier admirals. He was a year older than Spruance, and, like him, had started the war as the commander of a cruiser force, cruiser division 6.

Jack Fletcher knew the Pacific well, but, like Spruance and Nagumo, he had to learn about handling carriers the hard way: in command during a vital and confused battle. As the Coral Sea battle was the first carrier-to-carrier duel in the history of sea war Jack Fletcher learnt well, and learnt quickly.

The lessons he absorbed were that in such battles things not only moved very quickly but, more often than not, were not what they seemed. Fletcher's strategy had been dominated at Coral Sea by the determination that the Japanese invasion convoy heading for Port Moresby should not get through. It was to achieve this that he took the calculated risk of sending off his surface striking force on its own without air cover.

The highly inaccurate sighting reports and false claims made by the airmen of both sides at Coral Sea all made for a hazy and scrappy battle, but this was inevitable. Against such a background any criticism of Fletcher's operations must be muted.

In the end result, however, he was highly successful. True, in direct trade in terms of warship losses, he lost the valuable *Lexington* against a smaller Japanese carrier, but he hit both the larger Japanese carriers as well, in return for the damage to *Yorktown*. Much more important he handled his divided task forces skilfully and finally it was the Japanese that pulled out and that convoy never did get through to its objective.

Like others he had been accused of ultra-caution, but this hindsight judgement is unworthy. At Midway he was to utilise his limited forces with equal dexterity and not only did he show fine command in the placing of his ships for the combat, but he proved himself able to sum up a situation calmly. Although he was overall commander of the American ships at sea, at a vital juncture his readiness to hand over operational control to his subordinate stamped him as a shrewd and intelligent leader.

For the coming fight Fletcher had, to back up the *Yorktown*, only the tried and tested heavy cruisers *Astoria* and *Portland* with him plus a screen of six destroyers. Against Yamamoto's eleven battleships these forces would have no chance at all so it behove the Americans to keep their distance. The lack of screening ships was further accentuated by the decision, taken after much heart-searching, to send a task force to cover the Aleutians after all, albeit without a carrier. Two heavy cruisers, three light cruisers and ten destroyers were sent north under Rear Admiral Theobald. This decision resulted in a severe weakening of the already weak anti-aircraft screen of the carriers. In playing the Japanese at their own game in this way nothing was gained, for this force was unable to prevent the occupation of the Japanese objectives and would have been better utilised at Midway in the event. The Americans of course were far more vulnerable to diversification of their forces in this manner than the Japanese.

Other factors were to come into the delicate balance of this battle. The Japanese for instance were without radar (save for two experimental sets fitted in the battleships *Ise* and *Hyuga* just before they sailed). None of their search planes carried it of course, despite the recognition that early warning was now considered vital in the fast actions that developed with sea/air warfare.

The Americans were more fortunate in this respect. All three American carriers were fitted with radar as were some of their cruisers, including the new anti-aircraft cruiser which had just joined the fleet, the *Atlanta*. Midway island also had two search radars installed.

Lastly of course the United States task forces were fighting within 1000 miles of a fully equipped naval base which had just ably demonstrated its effectiveness. Thus any badly damaged ship stood a more than even chance of reaching home and, ultimately, rejoining the fight. The Japanese on the other hand were many thousands of miles from their home bases, and, to at least one major warship, this proved to be fatal.

Finally, in a similar manner to the Japanese and in the classic pattern for sea warfare, the Americans deployed a strong force of submarines to the east of the tiny atoll. No less than fifteen big boats were in positions east of Kure by the beginning of June, close enough in to the island target to ensure that every one of the Japanese battle groups would have to cross the sights of at least one of them.

Finally two seaplane tenders, *Thornton* and *Ballard*, together with an oiler and a destroyer and two auxiliary vessels, were sent out to the easternmost reefs and islands of the Hawaiian group in the French Frigate Shoals as aircraft rescue ships, and ten motor torpedo boats moved into Midway lagoon from Pearl Harbor to bolster the local defences.

Let us now examine these local defences. It will quickly become apparent that, despite its size, Midway, thanks to early appreciation of the Japanese intentions, was now becoming a very tough nut to crack indeed.

Examination of the map of the Pacific Ocean shows just how strategically important to the Americans Midway atoll was at this stage of the war. Situated 1135 miles from Pearl Harbor it commanded all the direct approaches to that base, now the only one available to the American fleet before the coast of California and the onrushing Japanese hordes.

Taking a broad sweep across the central Pacific it can be seen that its position was very vulnerable. Across the empty vastness of this great ocean nothing lay between it and Japan's home islands save for the even smaller Kure atoll a further sixty miles west. To the south-west lay the Marianas, heavily fortified by the Japanese and a major anchorage and staging post. Further round the huge arc of Japanese conquest lay the Marshall Islands and beyond them again the Solomons, where already the Japanese were established and building new airstrips in furtherance of the aim to sweep onward to Fiji and beyond. Even before the great Japanese armada had put to sea, plans had been discussed for them to go on to cover this next stage once Midway was occupied, as we have seen. To the north, the chilly and mist-shrouded Aleutians were another area where the Japanese would soon be firmly entrenched at Attu and Kiska. As outrider of that isolated Hawaiian chain, scattered like lonely stepping stones across the central Pacific, Midway atoll had a value out of all proportion to its actual area.

Only six miles in diameter, enclosed in a barrier reef, Midway had but two tiny scraps of inhabitable, treeless land. Sand Island, two miles long, is separated from Eastern Island, half that size, by a deep-water channel dredged to allow access to the inner lagoon where a fair-sized anchorage was available.

Eastern Island was almost entirely taken up by the triangular airstrip, the real objective of the actual assault, while on Sand Island lay most of the administrative and social buildings, a lighthouse, seaplane hangars and slip and the cable station. It had become an American possession in 1867 in one of those many quiet pieces of colonialism which America beat Britain to death with in her press but which, as with Panama and the Philippines among others, she indulged in whenever it suited her purpose. It had no importance at all for the first forty years of its new ownership but with the coming of the Pacific cable in the early 1900s it was officially named Midway and the marines, twenty strong, came ashore to guard it. Trans-Pacific clippers utilised it as a stop-over point and by 1940 the deep water channel had been completed.

Since that time work had gone on at an accelerated and, over the last month before June 1942, at a frenzied pace. Apart from a short bombardment on the night of 7 December 1941, by a brace of not very enthusiastic destroyers which caused little damage, Midway's defences had not been tested. Now there was a flurry of activity to make them invasion-proof.

Admiral Nimitz himself flew in in May to inspect progress. Under the joint control of the atoll commander, Commander

Cyril Simard and Lieutenant Colonel Harold Shannon of the Marine Corps, the defences were rapidly taking shape. Coastal defence batteries included some old 7in naval guns in blockhouses and there were adequate anti-aircraft guns in position, including 20mm bofors guns. A further battery of 37mm anti-aircraft guns arrived in May.

To reinforce the marine units already established on the atoll part of the 2nd Raider Battalion was landed, bringing the total complement of fighting men to 141 officers and 2886 men.

The air component was also reinforced. The Marine Corps had twenty Buffalo and seven Wildcat fighters of *VMF 221* under Major Floyd B. Parks, USMC, together with eleven Vindicator and sixteen Dauntless dive-bombers of *VMSB 241* under Major Lofton R. Henderson, Major Benjamin W. Norris and Captain Marshall A. Tyler, USMC.

Flying-boat detachments consisted of some thirty-two Catalinas from the navy and six of the brand-new Avenger torpedo-bombers of *VT 8* under Lieutenant L. K. Fieberling.

To these naval-orientated units the Army Air Force detachment of the VII Army Air Force, under Major General Willis P. Hale, added four twin-engined Marauder bombers under Captain James F. Collins and nineteen of the huge new four-engined B-17 Flying Fortresses under Lieutenant Colonel Walter C. Sweeney Jr and Major G. A. Blakey. The Army Air Force expected these big bombers to prove the decisive factor, but alas they merely took up a great deal of space and their contribution to the battle proved to be negligible.

Ashore, the 6th Marine Defense Battalion strung up wire and dug bomb-proof shelters while awaiting the arrival of the Japanese marines with whom they were eager to pay off old debts.

All were equally as confident at their chances as Shannon, who, when asked by Nimitz whether he could hold Midway against a major amphibious assault, replied, 'Yes, sir!'

Some examination of the types of aircraft the Americans were to use in the battle is of importance here for so much depended on them.

The front-line fighter of both the US Navy and Marine Corps was the sturdy, tubby little Grumman F4F Wildcat. With a wingspan of thirty-eight feet it was powered by a single Pratt and Whitney R-1830-76 Twin Wasp engine which gave it a top speed of 330 mph. It was armed with four 0.5in machine-guns in the wings, at a time when most fighters were switching over to cannon. It was therefore slower than the Japanese Zero and also less manoeuvrable.

The Buffalo was even more antiquated and had a top speed of only 313 mph. Its armament, of two 0.5in machine-guns, was woefully inadequate.

Likewise the Vindicator dive-bomber, although an advanced aircraft in its day, had had its day. Painfully slow and vulnerable it was gradually being phased out in favour of the Douglas SBD Dauntless. Perhaps the most effective naval dive-bomber of World War II, the Dauntless was, nonetheless, itself due for replacement. Its maximum speed was only 255 mph and its defensive armament consisted of two 0.5in machine-guns only, firing astern. It could carry a single heavy bomb. It was however universally popular with its crews and was particularly favoured for its ruggedness and reliability.

Among the torpedo-craft the Douglas Devastator was in the same position as the Vindicator in the dive-bombing field, obsolete but not yet replaced. With a speed never exceeding 225 mph the Devastator was literally a death trap when set upon by a Zero. It had a range of 980 miles and could carry a single 21in torpedo (carried at a unique angle, sloping down from the nose). Its replacement was the Grumman Avenger, designed to carry its torpedo internally. The TBF-1 combined the strike capacity of a twin-engined aircraft with the handiness and compactness of a carrier-based bomber and great things were expected of it. Maximum speed was 295 mph and it was powerfully and defensively armed with three 0.5in machine-guns and a 0.3in machine-gun. It could carry a single 22in torpedo or 2000 pounds of bombs. However it had not yet flown in actual combat.

The basic Japanese naval aircraft in these two categories, dive- and torpedo-bombing, were, as we have seen, the Kate and the Val. It was these two types of aircraft which had inflicted most of the carnage in the Pacific war up to this time, and, like the majority of the American types, both were nearing obsolescence by mid-1942. Both however had to soldier on since replacements were not initially forthcoming.

The Val dive-bomber was a two-seater with a maximum speed of 280 mph carrying a single 1050lb bomb. It was a monoplane but had a fixed undercarriage, similar to the German Junker 87 Stuka. Sharing this feature, it was likewise a strongly built aircraft but aerodynamically ugly. Its replacement was the Judy, but none were yet combat-ready in June 1942.

The Kate was a three-seater monoplane which carried its single torpedo, or 1100 pounds of bombs, externally. Single-engined, it had a maximum speed of only 225 mph and, like all torpedo-bombers, was exceedingly vulnerable to both fighters and anti-aircraft fire. Nonetheless the Kate was outstanding in its designed rôle and was one of the stalwarts of the Pacific War.

On the eve of battle it can be seen that both combatants had similar aircraft with similar faults and virtues. No one side could claim to have the monopoly in outdated material, no one side could state that the other lacked courage and determination. In numbers they were also fairly evenly matched in the skies, if not on the seas, thanks to Yamamoto's policy of dispersal. Only one element remained to be allocated among the opponents, luck. And, true to form, that very fickle lady switched her allegiance with startling rapidity during the battle which followed.

The actual composition of the American forces, as they slipped quietly out of Pearl Harbor at the end of May to face their mighty foe are contained in *Appendix Two* (page 185).

The stage was thus set, with many hundreds of thousands of tons of warships, hundreds of aircraft and several thousand soldiers, sailors and airmen concentrating to give battle for possession of a few square acres of sand and coral set in the middle of the world's largest ocean. Or so it appeared. But what was really at stake was the control of the whole of that broad ocean itself, and, ultimately, defeat or victory for the nations themselves.

The preliminary movements of these forces commenced with the sailing of the various submarine forces. At once the advantage of early intelligence of enemy movements played into the hands of the Americans, while over-confidence frustrated the Japanese dispositions.

The commander of the Pacific fleet submarines had been given ample opportunity to draw in distant units for the defence of their home base and a force of twenty-five boats was ready for duties along the likely approach routes of the enemy battle groups.

Rear Admiral English therefore sailed twelve of these, freshly refuelled and armed, to form the Midway patrol group west of the atoll in a crescent formation. A further group of three boats were given patrol areas closer in to Hawaii, between that section 200 miles to the north of Oahu and the area that provided any possible attack route swinging in from the north-west. Six others were allocated to the Aleutian operation, while the remaining four formed a more distant line to the north of Pearl Harbor. These movements were made between 21 and 24 May, so that all boats were in position well before the attack was due to take place.

Conversely the Japanese expected much from their own submarine arm, which had been especially trained to work in conjunction with the battle fleet against enemy warships rather than as a destroyer of merchant vessels similar to the German, British and Italian patterns.

Great reliance was therefore placed on the Japanese boats sighting the American forces coming up from Pearl and that, not only would they be able to pinpoint them for air strikes from the Nagumo carriers but they themselves might get in some heavy blows.

But all this depended on the Americans not reacting until Midway had been hit and occupied. Therefore, before the operation even commenced, the dispositions allocated to the strong Japanese submarine forces were outdated and useless. Worse still was the fact that even the original dates were not kept to.

It will be recalled that operation K was planned using two of the big Emily four-engined flying boats to make a last-minute scouting of Pearl Harbor on the eve of the operation using submarines for refuelling at French Frigate Shoals. However the

Americans had also decided that this group of islets, halfway along the chain from Oahu to Midway, would perform a similarly useful function and had already despatched the two old converted destroyers, *Ballard* and *Thornton*, to set up a seaplane base of their own. Moreover, because earlier Japanese activities from this position had not escaped the notice of the Americans, minefields had been laid and patrols by small fishing craft established to deny the Japanese a re-run.

Thus it was that, when the Japanese submarines forming the intended fuelling force arrived at French Frigate Shoals on the night of the 26 May, after calling at Kwajalein to pick up their cargo of aviation fuel and lubricating oils, they had an unpleasant surprise. *I-121* (Lieutenant Commander Fujimori) and *I-123* (Lieutenant Commander Ueno) were both mine-laying submarines especially adaptable for their new rôle, but they were impotent in the face of the established American presence.

Ueno immediately radioed back to his immediate superior at Kwajalein, Vice Admiral Goto, that the two American vessels ruled out the chance of carrying out the refuelling plan. Goto told Ueno to remain on watch in the area for a further twenty-four hours and hope that the two ships would leave before then, but obviously they did no such thing. Indeed their permanence at French Frigate Shoals was established beyond doubt when Ueno made further sightings of two Catalinas alighting there the next day. It was obvious that a seaplane base was in full operation and that therefore operation K must be abandoned completely.

I-122 (Lieutenant Commander Norita) had meantime been carrying out a reconnaissance of both Laysan and Lisianski Islands much further west along the chain, closer to Midway itself, but this did not prove to be the solution to the problem and Admiral Yamamoto was duly informed that operation K was cancelled. Although the three Japanese submarines spent a further three days among the shoals and islands they made no further contribution, although they were themselves not spotted.

This was a blow to the Japanese for it meant that no clear picture could be had of the actual composition of the American fleet as it lay at Pearl Harbor. Still it was not considered a major upset for they were still confident that the two submarine patrol lines, cordons A and B, would provide them with ample warning and details. But this too proved to be illusory.

The delay to operation K also meant that, in addition, *I-121*, *I-122* and *I-123* were late on station with cordon A, and they did not actually reach their stations until 4 June. To compound this delay, the boats forming cordon B had also sailed from their refitting ports late and could not now hope to be on call on 2 June as planned. Not until 3 June did they reach their patrol lines, far, far too late. In fact even had they got there on 2 June it would have made no difference, Spruance and Fletcher had long since passed on to the north. The Japanese submarine skippers patiently scanned the empty ocean in their wake. Aboard the *Yamato* and the *Akagi* their sighting reports were awaited in vain. Such was the start of the Japanese activities.

Admiral Spruance had departed from Pearl on 28 May with *Enterprise*, *Hornet*, five heavy cruisers, one anti-aircraft cruiser and his screen of nine destroyers. His orders were concise: he was to hold Midway and at the same time to inflict maximum damage on the enemy by strong attrition tactics.

Admiral Fletcher sailed in the *Yorktown*, with her patched-up hull and deck and her mixed and untrained aircrews. His orders were equally brief and to the point: he was to conduct target practice and then support task force 16.

Before they had left to take up their waiting positions some distance to the north-west of Midway, Admiral Nimitz had told them in his 'letter of instruction':

' . . . you will be governed by the principles of calculated risk, which you shall interpret to mean avoidance of exposure of your forces to attack by superior enemy forces without good prospect of inflicting, as a result of such exposure, greater damage on the enemy.'

Nimitz knew what was ploughing up from the west, he knew the magnitude of the task he was setting his two commanders. Whatever happened out there he knew that those handful of ships were all that he had. True, there were the seven old battleships under Admiral William S. Pye at San Francisco, together with the small escort carrier *Long Island*, but none of these ships could steam at more than twenty-one knots which was why he had left them there. True, their heavy anti-aircraft batteries would have helped but what was needed was speed and a long reach. Only the carriers had it, so (much to their intense disgust) the old battleships stayed put.

One further reinforcement which would have been invaluable was the mighty *Saratoga*, sister to the *Lexington*, eager to get into the scrap, but she could not make it. After picking up an escort she was steaming at full tilt towards Hawaii on 1 June, by which time it was already too late.

On 30 May Spruance refuelled from the *Cimarron* and *Platte* oiling force and the next day found the *Yorktown* force doing the same. Both task forces then rendezvoused on 2 June some 325 miles north-west of Midway atoll. It was planned that all initial air searches flown to locate the oncoming Japanese would be conducted by the land-based aircraft and the seaplanes. Thus the three American carriers would be able to keep their existence on the field of battle from the enemy until they themselves were ready to intervene. And Admiral Spruance was determined that the time for that was when Nagumo had shown his hand. Let him commit his aircraft to the Midway strike and then the American carriers would unleash their own attacks and hopefully catch the Japanese refuelling at their most vulnerable point.

However to do this he needed an early and precise fix as much as Yamamoto and Nagumo did. Like them he was not to receive any from his submarines, even though *they* were on time.

The American carriers nonetheless started to fly off their own air searches on 1 June in order that they themselves might not be surprised should the enemy change tactics. Both *Hornet* and *Enterprise* flew off search planes to the west and north-west over the next two days but without result. The two carrier groups and the attendant warships waited in keyed-up expectancy for the coming storm.

Robert Casey was a correspondent aboard one of the cruisers during the battle and the fact that everyone knew that, although

57

outnumbered, they had the drop on the enemy raised morale to a high pitch.

'The gunnery officer who until this moment has been un-enthusiastic about our mission in life is now talking about a possible annihilation of the Jap fleet,' he wrote. He also added prophetically, 'In naval war, apparently, you contrive to know not only where the other fellow is at all times, but what he's going to do. The process is ten per cent navigation and ninety per cent ouija board!'

Meanwhile from Midway itself, packed tight with troops, guns and aircraft, the tension was, if anything, at an even higher pitch. After all they were the target for all that consider-able hardware they knew the Japanese were sending and could expect, should things go ill at sea, visits from dive-bombers, heavy cruisers and crack Japanese marines, and all in a very short period. There was also the further interesting possibility of them being the first war-time live targets for the 18in guns of the *Yamato* should it prove that they were too tough for everything else.

The airstrip was packed with the huge bulks of the B-17s and the sleek shapes of the single-engined Wildcats and Buffalo fighters. The new forms of the Marauder twin-engined bombers and the Avengers showed that at last modern aircraft were arriving at the sharp end of the war.

Long-range air searches had been conducted without ceasing since 30 May by the two dozen Catalinas. These rugged old PBYs took off before light and pounded their way sluggishly out to cover the huge crescent sweeping from SSW to NNE at a range of 700 miles, well beyond the expected launching ranges of the Japanese carriers. Some of them ran into Japanese bombers from Wake Island and were badly cut up. The army's Fortresses, although not trained in sea searches, had the defen-sive armament to take care of themselves. They made a daily flight out to the reported rendezvous position of the Japanese forces, but they failed to sight anything at all during this period. Luck, at this stage of the operation, had befriended the Japanese, a bad weather front had reduced visibility to almost zero over a wide area and gave them a perfect approach blanket.

It also increased their confidence that they would arrive un-heralded.

The first of the Japanese groups to sail had been the Aleutians covering group of Rear Admiral Kakuta's second carrier striking force which had left the anchorage at Ominato, in northern Honshu, on 25 May and headed due east. The actual occupation convoys for Kiska, Addu and Attak sailed two days later, the former hugging the line of the Kurile Islands and the latter striking out north-east.

The bulk of the heavy ships assigned to act in the Midway drama sailed from the Bungo Straits and the Inland Sea, while the occupation force of Rear Admiral Tanaka, with Vice Admiral Kurita's heavy cruiser squadron and the minesweepers, departed from Saipan and Guam in the southern Marianas.

The final assessment of the Americans' defensive capability was made before these forces took departure, but it was remark-ably accurate considering the failure of any actual reconnais-sance contact.

The United States was estimated to have two or three aircraft-carriers, four or five heavy cruisers, three or four light cruisers, thirty destroyers and twenty-five submarines on hand, but no battleships. Save in a slight under-estimation on the heavy cruisers and an over-estimation on light cruisers, this was correct. When it came to assessing the defences of Midway atoll itself however, the Japanese calculations were more awry. They credited the shore-based marines with only 750 men, although acknowledging that these were fully equipped with coastal artillery and anti-aircraft guns.

On the vital point of air strength the Japanese gave figures well below actual numbers, some twelve army bombers and twenty fighters plus two dozen patrol planes was their guess. It was thought that once the initial strikes had gone in, these air-craft would be rapidly reinforced from Hawaii.

Before the actual sortie a final two-day period of exercises took place with the ships of the main and Kondo forces and the Nagumo carriers.

Nagumo's four big carriers sailed for the rendezvous with

fate on 26 May and these were followed, next day, by the grim bulks of the battleships, their first wartime sortie since the early months of the war. Bristling with guns and looking unassailable in their might, their crews celebrated their chance to take part in annihilation of the enemy by cheering and singing as they went.

Happy as the men of the Imperial Navy were to be going in to battle, their superiors were not quite so enthusiastic. Admiral Yamamoto himself had a stomach complaint, while the always stolid and unemotional Nagumo was unhappy at the pace of the preparations forced upon his already weary force. One eye-witness described the Admiral at this time as: '. . . warm-hearted and sympathetic as ever, but his once-vigorous fighting spirit seemed to be gone, and with it his stature as an outstanding naval leader. Instead he seemed rather average, and I was suddenly aware of his increased age.'

The main force soon began to approach the bad weather area, strong head winds whipped up heavy seas which caused them to reduce speed to fourteen knots to help the ships of the destroyer screen maintain formation. The weather continued to deteriorate the following day, 2 June.

Many hundreds of miles to the east the big carriers had also run into the dismal weather, with low clouds and drizzle, but for them it was a godsend and could be endured. Their only fear was that it would not clear in time for their first strikes to go off as planned.

Down to the south the occupation convoy was making its way up from Guam, with Kurita's four powerful cruisers and two destroyers riding point some 100 miles ahead of them with the seaplane carriers following in the rear. It was from this group that the first signs began to manifest themselves that the Americans might not, after all, be completely asleep.

Messages picked up by the radio room of the flagship *Yamato* strongly pointed to the fact that a strong American patrol line of submarines was already operating on the approach route the occupation force was taking to its objective. Opinions began to be expressed that the convoy had been sighted and that, should this be the case, the Americans must deduce what their objective was and be alerted. However the prevailing view was that this was merely guesswork, and, even if true, not too alarming. It would merely mean that the American fleet would be drawn out exactly as intended, there was still time for Midway to fall.

Indeed, even after these reports, no change in plan was thought necessary, the big ships plunged on in the gloom ever eastward. The battleships and carriers began to refuel in the murk in readiness for the final stage. Their target to the east, by contrast, lay basking in brilliant warm sunshine. Only the ships of the occupation force were spared the gloomy but welcome cloud cover and this proved to be the first point of contact between the two sides.

The ships of the Midway occupation force were steaming in two parallel columns at an estimated speed of nineteen knots. Ahead and between the two columns' line of advance steamed the light cruiser *Jintsu*, flying the flag of Rear Admiral Tanaka, with the eight destroyers of the escort spread in a semi-circle ahead, the destroyer *Hayashio* astern and the two seaplane tenders stationed on either side of the main force. Separate from this group were the minesweepers of Captain Miyamoto's group with their attendant patrol craft and it was actually this small force which was first sighted by the questing American PBYs at 0848 on the morning of 3 June. A short time later another Catalina piloted by Ensign Jack Reid broke through the clouds at the end of his timed run in readiness to turn back after another fruitless search. Suddenly, laid out before him like models, lay the ships of the invasion convoy.

Reid commenced to shadow the convoy sending back his sighting reports as he did so. For several hours he clung to the coat-tails of the Japanese force, estimating its strength at eleven ships, its speed at nineteen knots and its course straight for Midway atoll! Tanaka, still 600 miles from his objective, was justifiably enough annoyed. Aboard the transports the Japanese marines had been undertaking final preparations and drills for the assault, now all felt naked and exposed. Kurita's comforting heavy cruisers were miles away out of sight, no help could be expected from them. He signalled Yamamoto the bad news and then tried to drive off the persistent shadower with gunfire, but he was not initially successful.

Back at Midway the long-awaited news galvanised the tiny

airstrip into fresh activity. At last there was something tangible to cope with instead of rumours and scares. Action was swift, Commander Simard ordering immediate air strikes against the convoy. Bombs loaded and ready, nine of the giant B-17s rolled down the strip and climbed into the western sky. The drone of their four great engines died into a muffled beat as they disappeared over the horizon. The Army Air Force was supremely confident that these great aircraft would be perfectly capable of dealing with any threat from the sea; the shades of Billy Mitchell hung around the nine big ships as they thundered towards the plodding merchant ships.

At 1624 they found them, some 570 miles from Midway and still holding their steady course. The guns of the escorts began to wink as if in greeting but the Fortresses carried out their attacks far out of range of the puny anti-aircraft weapons of the Japanese boats. In three waves, at heights between 8000 and 12,000 feet, they released their bomb loads. Far below the sea boiled and heaved as the bombs exploded, but the nearest was 1000 metres from any ship of the force and the convoy continued on its dogged way unscathed.

Not for the last time the Army Air Force flyers returned with fantastic claims of their own successes. Two battleships or heavy cruisers had received direct hits, they stated at the debriefing, and at least two of the transports! The American submarine *Cuttlefish* (Lieutenant Commander Hottel), on her lonely beat some 650 miles west of Midway was ordered to conduct a search for these crippled heavy units. One of the oldest and slowest submarines in the American navy the *Cuttlefish* was delighted to be offered such juicy targets and set to work with a will. Considering that all the B-17s had hit was empty water it is not surprising that her diligence went unrewarded.

The next shore-based strike directed at the occupation force was less spectacular both in its composition and numbers. Four Catalinas, armed with an aerial torpedo each, were sent off to make a night attack on the convoy. They ran down the approach route at their best speed and were rewarded with a radar sighting at 0015 on the 4th.

They found the convoy illuminated in bright moonlight and three of the PBYs were able to launch their torpedoes at the solid mass of shipping and escape unscathed. One of their missiles struck home, hitting the rear ship of the port column, the oiler *Akebono Maru*. The torpedo detonated close to the ship's bows and the explosion killed eleven sailors and injured a further thirteen. But despite this her watertight bulkheads held fast and she was able to report to Rear Admiral Tanaka that she could maintain her place in the convoy line without difficulty. News of this second strike was radioed to Yamamoto; the convoy continued to steadily close the miles between itself and its destination. For the four PBYs their adventures were not yet over. Having made the first hit on a Japanese ship in this battle, and duly escaped from the flak, they set course back for Midway. The ancient amphibians lumbered on through the night and arrived over the atoll just in time to witness the first Japanese bombs bursting. It would have been suicide to attempt to put down so they headed out for quieter waters, eventually putting down at Laysan and Lisianski Islands. They had been in the air for thirteen hours.

The startling news of the discovery of the Japanese force approaching Midway from the south-west was confirmation that all their intelligence work was spot-on. However the information received from the Army flyers that the force contained battleships and liners, 'about the size of the *Normandie*' (one of the largest ships afloat!) gave rise to doubts about their estimates of the actual composition of the Japanese forces. For a time the occupation force was considered to be nothing less than the main force and various American dispositions began to be changed to meet this new situation.

Up at Point 'Luck', to the north-west of Midway, some 300 miles from the atoll and (unknown to them), 400 miles east of the oncoming Japanese carrier force, Admiral Fletcher took in this actual sighting and attack reports and had to balance them with the very precise guesses on which his present position was based. He quite correctly deduced that these air sightings were highly coloured and that what had in fact been sighted was the duly expected invasion force consisting solely of transports and light escorts.

This being so he saw no reason to alter his intentions and, at 1950 on 3 June, the three American carriers came round on a southerly course and steamed through the night to a position some 200 miles due north of Midway. From this position he hoped to be able to launch his strikes at Nagumo whom he was certain was still coming in from the north-west. The bad weather front was still shielding the Japanese from him, but he was equally certain that his carriers also were completely unknown to his enemy. In both assumptions Fletcher was absolutely correct.

Meanwhile the Japanese carrier admiral was making equally profound statements after a similar period of anxiety following the attacks on the occupation force. As has already been noted Nagumo was far from happy with the way things had been conducted up to now, nor was he one hundred per cent pleased with the performance of his new aircrew. However none of these doubts prevented him from feeling completely confident in his command's ability to carry out the assignments given to it. This is all the more remarkable when one realises that the four carriers of the Nagumo force had been given orders for 4 June that were almost diametrically opposite to each other and that he had to pursue both these objectives simultaneously.

His main aim was stated to be the complete destruction of any American surface fleet that ventured out to oppose him, especially the destruction of the American aircraft-carriers. To do this he would need every one of his fighters, both for defence of his own carriers should they be attacked, and to escort his torpedo- and dive-bombers in their strikes against the enemy. But his first objective had been laid down as nothing less than ' . . . an aerial attack on Midway', in order to annihilate all enemy air forces stationed there. Now the versatility of the carrier-based aircraft is that it could carry out both these functions, *given time*. For the attack on Midway airfield, torpedoes were obviously useless and his Kates would have to be armed with bombs. But against enemy carriers and warships torpedoes were essential and his aircraft would have to be re-armed, and rearmed quickly.

Midway atoll showing the vital airstrips for which this decisive battle was fought
COURTESY OF NATIONAL ARCHIVES

The Avenger torpedo-bomber which made its debut at this battle and sustained terrible losses
COURTESY OF NATIONAL ARCHIVES

Rear Admiral Frank Fletcher, the commander of the US Task Forces in the battle
COURTESY OF NATIONAL ARCHIVES

Rear Admiral Chester W. Nimitz whose patient planning and careful preparations led to the convincing American victory
COURTESY OF NAVAL HISTORY DIVISION, FADM NIMITZ COLLECTION

USS *Hornet,* one of the three American carriers which took part in the battle
COURTESY OF NATIONAL ARCHIVES

Admiral Chuichi Nagumo, the commander of the Japanese carrier group that bore the brunt of the battle
COURTESY OF NAVAL HISTORY DIVISION

Admiral Isoroku Yamamoto who planned and masterminded the Japanese attack
COURTESY OF NAVAL HISTORY DIVISION

Devastator torpedo-bombers on the deck of the USS *Yorktown*
COURTESY OF NATIONAL ARCHIVES

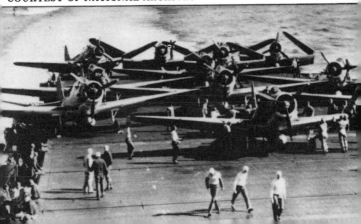

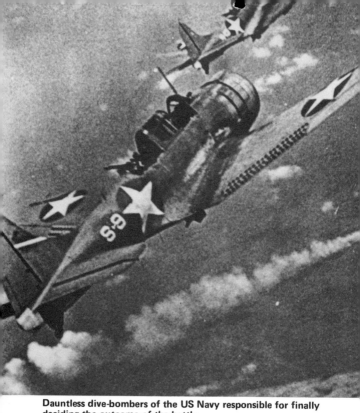

Dauntless dive-bombers of the US Navy responsible for finally deciding the outcome of the battle
COURTESY OF NATIONAL ARCHIVES

The stricken carrier *Yorktown* listing alarmingly after suffering severe damage
COURTESY OF NATIONAL ARCHIVES

But time was one thing the Japanese were certain they had ample measure of. It was their operation on ground of their own choosing. So confident was Nagumo that he was still to have at least a whole day to complete the first part of his operation before turning to the second that, on the eve of the battle, he issued the following estimation to his commanders:

1 The enemy fleet will probably come out to engage when the Midway landing operations are begun.
2 Enemy air patrols from Midway will be heavier to westward and southward, less heavy to the north and northwest.
3 The radius of enemy air patrols is estimated to be approximately 500 miles.
4 The enemy is not yet aware of our plan, and he has not yet detected our task force.
5 There is no evidence of an enemy task force in our vicinity.
6 It is therefore possible for us to attack Midway, destroy land-based planes there, and support landing operations. We can then turn around, meet an approaching enemy task force, and destroy it.
7 Possible counter attacks by enemy land-based aircraft can surely be repulsed by our interceptors and anti-aircraft fire.

On every one of these points except no 7 Admiral Nagumo was wrong. If Admiral Fletcher can be said to have correctly estimated his opponent's moves with uncanny accuracy and skill, Admiral Nagumo's guessing about how the battle was at that moment shaping must stand out as the classic case of inaccuracy and over-confidence on record!

Nor was he alone in this. Many miles astern the battleships of the Kondo force were preparing to part company with *Yamato* and her consorts and sail away to the north-east. The combined fire-power of this squadron was capable of destroying the entire strength of the American navy west of Hawaii with ease, providing it came within range. The shells of the *Yamato* herself could be flung with accuracy for twenty-five miles. Her distance from Fletcher's force that night was over five hundred miles. Not only was the colossal fire-power of this squadron thus made impotent, but the tremendous weight of anti-aircraft fire-power these great ships could throw up was equally lost in the impending duel. And finally there is the consideration of the splitting of the weight of the attacking bombers which the presence of these great ships would provide, if nothing else. Although briefed to attack the Japanese carriers only, the temptation to release torpedoes at such promising targets as the battleships may well have proved irresistible to some pilots.

Aboard one of the occupation force's escorting destroyers, Commander Tameichi Hara was reflecting the faith which they all still had of certain victory in the morning. He was to write:

'We were well aware that we were advancing against a fully prepared enemy, but I was no longer ill at ease. The attempts thus far against our convoy had been furtive and feeble. The Nagumo task force could smash the enemy with its sledge-hammer blows.'

Thus the final hours of darkness passed and the dawn of 4 June broke, the last dawn for more than two thousand men.

CHAPTER THREE

THE GIANT STRIKES

The big carriers of the Nagumo force had reached their planned flying-off position for the launching of the first attack on Midway atoll undetected by 0430 on the morning of 4 June. Although the heavy cloud which had hitherto protected this force was beginning to break up into patchy cover and the wind was still slight for flying-off operations, fortune, it was felt, was still with the attackers. Not only would they be able to launch their aircraft as scheduled against their unsuspecting enemy, but there still remained a good chance of them continuing to evade detection themselves. Further east, skies were clearer and therefore their own air searches ought to be rewarded with better success should the Americans venture forth as hoped.

At 0430 then, the muffled silence that had hitherto accompanied the passage of these great ships of war was broken by the harsh and strident snarls of aircraft engines as the leading planes warmed up and went roaring off the great wooden flight decks into the indigo sky. The green take-off lamps glowed and the Zero fighters trundled down *Akagi*'s flight deck one after the other, accompanied by the cheers and happy shouts of the crew. The day of decision had come.

The fleet was some 240 miles north-west of Midway and dawn was half an hour away as these aircraft of the first wave took to the air. Under the command of Lieutenant Joicho Tomonaga of the *Hiryu* the total strength of this great air armada was thirty-six Kate bombers from *Soryu* and *Hiryu*, acting in their level bombing rôle this time and each armed with one externally slung 800kg bomb for use against land targets.

They were quickly joined by the thirty-six Val dive-bombers

TAKASU
4 BATTLESHIPS
2 CRUISERS
12 DESTROYERS

NAGUMO
4 CARRIERS
2 BATTLESHIPS
3 CRUISERS
11 DESTROYERS

YAMAMOTO
3 BATTLESHIPS
1 CARRIER
3 CRUISERS
9 DESTROYERS

NAUT

US SHORE-
BASED AIR
ATTACKS HIT
0630-0830

KONDO
2 BATTLESHIPS
1 CARRIER
5 CRUISERS
8 DESTROYERS

TANAKA
CONVOY
1 CRUISER
8 DESTROYERS

KURITA
4 CRUISERS
2 DESTROYERS

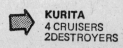

MIDWAY 1
APPROX POSITIONS
OF MAIN FORCES ON
EARLY MORNING OF
4th JUNE 1942
FIRST AIR STRIKES

NOT TO SCALE

FLETCHER
1 CARRIER
2 CRUISERS
6 DESTROYERS

SPRUANCE
2 CARRIERS
6 CRUISERS
9 DESTROYERS

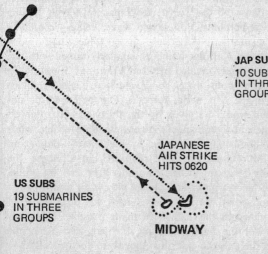

JAP SUBS
10 SUBMARINES
IN THREE
GROUPS

JAPANESE
AIR STRIKE
HITS 0620

US SUBS
19 SUBMARINES
IN THREE
GROUPS

MIDWAY

from *Akagi* and *Kaga*, under command of Lieutenant Shoichi Ogawa, each carrying its single 250kg bomb between the stubby undercarriage spats.

Once airborne they were joined by their fighter cover, the thirty-six Zero fighters of Lieutenant Masaharu Suganami from *Soryu*. This dense mass of fighting aircraft circled for a short while over the fleet, sorting themselves into formation then, to the cheers being renewed on the now-empty flight decks, they took their departure towards far-distant Midway.

Almost immediately, as the first light crept up over the horizon, the carriers became the scene of renewed and frenzied activity. First of all, more Zero fighters came up from below on the massive lifts of the *Kaga*. These soon took off, nine in all, to form a standing air combat patrol over the Nagumo force. Another flight on the deck of the *Akagi* was spotted ready to relieve them. A total of eighteen fighters to protect the whole fleet seemed a small number, but there was still no hint or sign of any American reaction. Should any develop from the east then Nagumo would be ready for them. Again the gongs sounded and the giant lifts rose up from the hangar levels bringing with them the second wave of bombers and escorts.

Under the overall command of Lieutenant Commander Takashige Egusa of the *Soryu*, the Japanese Navy's leading expert in dive-bombing, this second wave, being prepared to sortie out against any American carrier force, comprised a further thirty-six Val dive-bombers, similarly armed with one 250kg bomb, equally divided between *Hiryu* and *Soryu*, while on the decks of both *Akagi* and *Kaga* were ranged eighteen Kates carrying a 24in aerial torpedo. Fighter cover for this second group would be given by the thirty-six Zero fighters under Lieutenant Commander Shigeru Itaya of *Akagi*, while the torpedo-bomber force was led by Lieutenant Commander Shigeharu Murata of the same ship. All in all these 108 combat-ready aircraft, silently awaiting their call to action, represented the cream of the Japanese Navy's air arm. By their actions, more than anything else, had the tidal wave of Japanese victory to this date been made possible. Now they were eager for the final reckoning. If there were American carriers out there to the east, then they were doomed ships!

In order to ascertain whether the Americans had laid on any sort of reception committee, although it was a probability that was hardly given serious thought by Nagumo, aerial searches were to be carried out by the seaplanes carried by the heavy ships of the Nagumo force's escort.

In addition to a single aircraft from each of the big carriers, *Akagi* and *Kaga*, Vals to patrol the southern sectors of his line of advance, the heavy cruisers *Chikuma* and *Tone* were both to launch their Pete navy-type observer seaplanes from their catapults to search the eastern arcs for a depth of some 300 miles, while the battleship *Haruna* sent off its more elderly Dave floatplane to supplement these searches by carrying out a 150-mile sweep inside the others' arcs. If anything was moving out there these aircraft would be able to report it in good time for the second wave to deal with it.

Unfortunately for the Japanese these seaplane searches were singularly ineffective. The *Tone* aircraft could not be launched until 0500, half an hour later than planned, due to a fault with the launching catapult. No other aircraft was substituted to take her place. That from the *Chikuma* got airborne on time but with engine trouble.

This aircraft limped away on its course with spluttering motor and its crew, already preoccupied with this, were further hampered by a patch of bad weather and turbulence. At 0635 it was forced to return. Its crew reported that they had seen nothing at all on their outward leg. The convictions of the Japanese commanders received a further assurance. Everything was going splendidly!

But the crew of *Chikuma*'s floatplane had been terribly wrong. There *was* something moving out there in her sector and she had flown right over it. Fletcher and his three big carriers were out there, and ready for action.

Over the two American task groups the dawn of this fatal 4 June broke with still airs and good visibility. About the same time as the first bombers from the Japanese ships had struck out for Midway as a vast mass of black dots, the *Yorktown* was launching the first of her Dauntless dive-bombers to undertake scouting missions to the west. In all she put ten aircraft into the early-morning air to cover a large semi-circle 100 miles out from the task force.

At this point in time Nagumo's four carriers and Admiral Fletcher's three were about 215 miles apart and on slightly converging courses. None of *Yorktown*'s questing dive-bombers therefore came across the Japanese fleet which was still partially hidden by broken cloud. The airwaves remained chillingly silent as Fletcher awaited the first positive sighting of his powerful adversary which he was certain was just over the horizon.

This was the first of many crises to be faced and questions to be asked. Would the Japanese show their hand as expected by hitting Midway first, or what if they should have already sighted Fletcher's own ships and even now be outflanking him from the north? Even now a deadly wave of dive- and torpedo-bombers might be winging in to assail his formation, silently and expectantly steaming south-west in two squadrons, just in sight of each other.

Reaching the end of their 100-mile legs the Dauntless bombers began to turn back, some having penetrated the northern fringes of the towering cloud formations shielding Nagumo. They had nothing to report. The clocks ticked on quietly, the tension rose another notch.

On Midway atoll itself, 0430 had seen the despatch of a fourth group of aerial searchers; eleven of the navy Catalinas rolled across the lagoon and heaved their sluggish bulks into the air and panted heavily out towards the western horizon.

An hour passed and aboard the Catalina of flight 58 anxious eyes tried to penetrate the murk below them.

At 0530 precisely Lieutenants Howard Ady and William Chase nosed their PBY through a break in the clouds and far below was sighted the trailing wake of a surface vessel at speed. Banking to the north and dropping down through the cloud they spotted a second wake and then others, within seconds they were in view of the empty decks of two of the Japanese carriers.

At the same time lookouts aboard the Japanese task force heard the muffled beating of the Catalina and then spotted it slipping through the clouds like a bird of ill-omen. Immediately alarm bells rang out, gunners cranked their sighting wheels and the barrels of a score or more anti-aircraft guns turned towards the lumbering American floatplane and elevated. With a succession of cracks, heavy and light weapons aboard the nearest ships began to hammer away.

Ignoring the bursts of ugly black smoke that began to blossom all around them, the American pilots soared right across the Japanese fleet and swung back up into the clouds astern. Pilots hastily manned their aircraft and Zeros snarled off the decks of all four Japanese carriers in order to catch and destroy the Catalina. In vain! The PBY had slipped back into the cloud cover and successfully evaded all attempts to intercept her.

At 0534 came the words for which every American had been waiting so tensely: 'Enemy carriers.'

That was all but it was enough to finally confirm all their guesses and hunches. Together with the earlier location of the invasion force it meant that all the pieces of the complicated jigsaw, they had been assembling blindfold, were now falling into place precisely as predicted.

Within minutes Catalina 58 was amplifying her initial sighting with reports on the enemy air strike now en route to Midway:

'Many planes heading Midway, bearing 320°, distance 150.'

So Nagumo *had* committed himself to the first strike. Admiral Fletcher could not have had better news. What was needed to fit the final piece into place was the precise location of the Japanese vessels. At 0603 he got just that. A second Catalina, flight 92, joined the first in the complicated game of hide and seek with the Zeros. She signalled:

'Two carriers and battleships bearing 320°, distance 180, course 135, speed 25.'

This put the ships of the Nagumo force about 200 miles WSW of Fletcher's force. True, it was actually out by 40 miles but it was near enough to matter. The Americans now knew the location of their major foe, and, as further PBYs began to home in, they were certain of maintaining that surveillance with increasing accuracy. They themselves however still remained unlocated.

Now was the time to strike. But before he could take the *Yorktown* into the fight, Fletcher had to recover his scouting planes. This would cause an unacceptable delay, during which time all his own advantage of surprise would be lost. Fletcher therefore signalled to Rear Admiral Spruance to take *Enterprise*, *Hornet* and their escorts and steam south-west. His final command was precise: 'Attack enemy carriers when definitely located.' As soon as he had recovered his aircraft he would bring the *Yorktown* group up in support.

Visibility was now some fifty miles around the American ships with a light sea. The big carriers soon began to work up to twenty-five knots and up on to their decks came their own aircraft. In a repetition of what had taken place aboard the Japanese ships two hours earlier the deck parks began to fill up with roaring fighters, dive-bombers and torpedo planes.

Meanwhile, from Midway itself, powerful air striking forces were already airborne.

The first of these were the sixteen B-17 Fortresses of flight 92, which had actually taken off before dawn to carry out further attacks against the slow-moving transports of the Japanese invasion convoy, which were still doggedly holding their course up from the south-west, despite the hammering they were supposed to have undergone.

Under the command of Lieutenant Colonel Walter C. Sweeney, USA, these big planes were already well en route when the first sighting reports of the Nagumo force came in. There was no question of them continuing on their original mission. The obvious priority target for every aircraft that could fly was the Japanese carriers. Admiral Nimitz back at Pearl Harbor signalled to Simard to leave the defence of the islands to their own anti-aircraft guns and, 'go all out for the carriers'. Accordingly Sweeney was instructed to swing north and join in the all-out assault against Nagumo.

On the atoll itself the striking forces had been at instant readiness and it took very little time for them all to get into the sky. This was vital for, at 0550, the shore-based radar stations on the atoll began reporting their own confirmations of the PBYs' warnings. Heavy incoming groups of hostile aircraft were located, moving fast, some 93 miles out and closing rapidly. The air raid sirens began to wail out and gunners tumbled into their positions. Already the little airstrip was alive with planes moving out before they got caught on the ground. There was to be no second Pearl Harbor at Midway!

The first aircraft to get away were the sixteen Marine Corps Dauntless dive-bombers of Major Lofton Henderson, USMC. Each was carrying a 500lb bomb as they swarmed into the sky and headed west. They were followed by the eleven Vindicator dive-bombers of Major Benjamin W. Norris, known fondly as 'Vibrators'.

Dive-bombing was known to be the most accurate form of aerial attack at this stage of the war but, as already related, the Vindicators were the oldest aircraft in the fleet and were terribly slow. The Dauntless crews, although having more modern aircraft under them, were handicapped by the fact that they had never before flown a Dauntless prior to their flight to Midway, and no training could be carried out owing to the accidental destruction of much of their aviation fuel! In view of this, Henderson decided to carry out his attack by the simpler method of glide-bombing from a less acute angle. Although making less demands on his fresh crews this method unfortunately would prolong their approach time in the face of alerted defences. Nonetheless this seemed the best chance for Henderson's unit.

The dive-bombers were followed by the torpedo-bombers. This was certainly the most positive way of putting down heavy warships, but it was also the most dangerous form of attack for the flyers too. It required absolute steadiness in approach at very low level thus giving the gunners on the defending warships ample time for accurate, nil-deflection shots. It also meant that no evasive action could be taken if they were attacked by defending fighters. It took a very special courage to be a torpedo-bomber pilot.

Four of these were the new B-26 twin-engined bombers of the Army Air Force, under Captain James F. Collins, making their operational début in this rôle in the war. The Martin Marauder was a seven-seater light attack bomber with a speed of 284 mph and a range of 1000 miles. It was defensively armed with eleven machine-guns and fitted to carry a 22in aerial torpedo internally. Its sleek aerodynamic shape had earned it the nickname 'Flying Torpedo' when it first appeared, a name which was later changed to the more chilling one of 'Widow Maker', due to a high percentage of flight accidents during subsequent operations.

These were joined by the six new Avengers of *VT-8*, led by Lieutenant Langdon K. Fieberling, again making an operational début in hardly ideal conditions.

An essential factor in aerial attack against strong warship formations was the need to synchronise all arms in order to confuse and swamp the defences. In this case no such synchronisation was even attempted, the planes took off as they could and each group headed towards the Japanese fleet at their own best, and widely varying, speeds. Thus there was no mutual support. Even more tragic was the fact that, despite Admiral Nimitz's instructions to rely solely on anti-aircraft defences, the total strength of the Midway fighter defences were held back to engage the oncoming Japanese air strike, as they did not have the range to accompany the American strike aircraft anyway.

Accordingly the twenty obsolete Buffalo and the six serviceable Wildcats of the Marine Corps were vectored out in two groups in defence of their airfield. The larger group of Japanese Zeros outmatched both these types as well as outnumbering them. Nevertheless they were all there was. The American Interceptors climbed away in two separate groups of thirteen, Major Floyd B. Parks leading his section straight at the oncoming Japanese formation, while Major Kirk Armistead took his section out to the west to prevent any outflanking move by the enemy. But at 0615, when Parks's small group sighted the Japanese hordes approaching in their rigid formations of 'Vee of Vees' with the dark cloud of Zeros above them, Armistead's section was ordered to close Parks, and together the marines swept towards Tomonaga's horde.

At 0616 the marine fighters, reduced to twenty-five when one fighter developed engine defects and was forced to return, started to climb to 17,000 feet ahead of the Japanese air armada. The actual strength of this force was over-estimated by the defenders to be some eighty bombers and fifty fighters, but, even at its true strength, the odds were formidable enough.

Parks got his 5000-feet height advantage over the leading bombers and commenced his attack with his twelve fighters. Too far astern to immediately give him support Armistead's thirteen Interceptors were struggling to close. As Parks's formation pushed over, Lieutenant Suganami's first flights pulled effortlessly up to head them off, displaying a speed and flexibility that left the Americans powerless.

Within seconds there was a fierce, confused and pitiless dogfight in progress. Despite all their efforts, neither Parks nor Armistead could break through to the Japanese bomber formations and they themselves were soon in big trouble as the Zeros latched on to their tails and the chatter of machine-gun fire rattled out over the empty ocean.

It did not last long, this first onslaught. Outnumbered and outflown, there was nothing that the marine flyers' gallantry could do to redress the situation. Soon the skies were filled with flaming Buffalo fighters and the explosions of disintegrating aircraft.

Within a few minutes thirteen Buffalo fighters and two Wildcats had been shot down. Among those who failed to return was the gallant Parks who led the hopeless fight with courage. Despite claims of heavy Japanese losses in return, only two Zero fighters were destroyed in this attack, and these, it was estimated, fell victim to the atoll's anti-aircraft guns later.

Meanwhile, unaffected by the swirling combat taking place above and then behind them, the bombers of the Japanese force sped on towards their target. It was very soon apparent to them, however, that they hit an empty larder. The most important part of their objective had been to destroy the atoll's air striking power, and although the American fighters had been almost wiped out, the bombers had gone.

Both Ogawa and Tomonaga had no choice but to concentrate on what worthwhile targets remained in the shape of the island's runways, oil storage tanks, barracks and coastal batteries. The high-flying level formation of Kates arrived over the atoll, at 0628, at a height of 14,000 feet. They concentrated their attack on the airstrips of Eastern Island.

Ogawa's dive-bombers, robbed of their true prey, turned to the shore installations and tipped over to commence their screaming dives. Anti-aircraft fire laced up to meet them as the fully prepared defenders hit back hard. Six 3in guns opened their barrage against the high-altitude Kates. But maintaining their steady and predictable course in the face of this vicious fire, as it was later described, they provided relatively simple targets for the guns to lock on to and soon no less than three were hit, bursting into flames and spiralling to the sea below in long trails of smoke and flames.

The Vals however were a different proposition. All available short-range guns burst into life as they barrelled down out of the smoky sky at full throttle: 20mm guns, light machine-guns, all commenced a bedlam of sound and fury as they tried to halt the seemingly irresistible power dives of Ogawa's men. In the lagoon several of the little PT boats (Motor Torpedo Boats), had got underway and were spiralling around the calm waters in a frenzy of spray while their own little guns joined in the general barrage.

With the noise of this barrage, the pandemonium of the Vals as they levelled out at almost nought feet over their targets, and crunch and blast of the heavy bombs bursting among the sand dunes and coral, the tiny atoll represented a scene from hell.

A Val was caught in a cross-fire and disintegrated in mid-air, an awesome funeral pyre for three Japanese flyers. Their own fight over, the Zero fighters joined in the main attack, making low-level strafing runs across the islands, their machine-guns kicking up bursts of sand and rock in long parallel lines of death. Incendiary bullets turned block houses and oil storage tanks into blazing infernos.

Within seventeen minutes the violence and the fury was over and the Japanese aircraft were winging their way back to their home carriers and silence again fell on the lonely atoll. Behind them they left a pall of smoke rising into the still Pacific air from the burnt-out and gutted remnants of the oil tanks on Sand Island. It remained for the defenders to count the cost of this hot little action.

The loss of the fuelling system was a blow, and what few fighters remained on hand to deal with any subsequent attacks would have to be refuelled slowly by hand methods. The sea-plane hangar and the hospital were both completely wrecked by direct hits and many of the store houses were also completely demolished. The Japanese efforts to crater the airfield runways were not so successful however and the strips remained operational. Nor were the radar installations put out of action and the cable station was also spared. Indeed so ineffectual was the attack on the airfield that some American observers thought that this may have been deliberate policy in order that the Japanese themselves could quickly make use of them when they came ashore to set up shop!

Wild claims as to the damage they had inflicted upon the attacking aircraft were to be mirrored in most of the subsequent action reports of that day. No less than fifty-three Japanese aircraft were claimed as destroyed when in fact total losses by Tomonaga's force was six aircraft, all these to surface fire. On the other hand the Japanese airmen were equally wild for they claimed the destruction of no less than forty-two American fighters!

When the skies were clear the American fighters were told to land. Pitifully few of them remained to comply with that order. Seventeen had been shot down and of those that survived to stumble back to Midway with torn and ripped aircraft, seven were damaged beyond repair. The total available fighter strength remaining to the marines, in the likely event of a second air attack on the scale of the first, was five fighters!

Despite this it was clear to Tomonaga that this initial air strike against a forewarned defence was not a success. The anti-aircraft and shore batteries were still largely untouched and it was obviously essential that a further attack be mounted to reduce the island garrison still further before the Japanese marines could storm ashore there. Accordingly at 0700, while making his way back to Nagumo, Tomonaga radioed:

'There is need for a second attack.'

But over the horizon Nagumo was having problems of his own.

Almost at the same time as the Japanese bombers were arriving over the empty Midway airstrips seeking the American strike aircraft, the first scattered groups of these had located Nagumo's task force and were commencing their own counter attacks.

Apart from the still-persistent and still-elusive PBYs the Japanese carrier force had still seen no sign of American opposition when Tomonaga's signal was received. But within five minutes of his recommendation being taken in by *Akagi*, and while the decision was still being made whether or not to risk complying with it, the first of the incoming waves of American bombers was sighted by one of the leading destroyers and the whole fleet started to manoeuvre in anticipation of heavy attacks.

As the first American aircraft were sighted coming in fast from the port bow the escorting destroyers on that side of the screen opened up a long-range barrage with their dual-purpose long-barrelled 5in guns. But they only fired a few rounds before they stopped. The reason was clear enough: the Zeros of the standing air patrol were in among the enemy and inflicting great carnage.

From the wave-hopping level at which the American planes were approaching it was soon plain that these were torpedo-bombers. The protecting Zeros made their interceptions well out from the fleet and little could at first be made out from the Japanese warships other than the distant chatter of machine-guns, the blossoming plume of dark smoke smudged against the distant sea and the brief splash as the fire-encased bombers were engulfed by the ocean.

It would appear that the four Marauders and the six Avengers had kept more or less in company during their long, lonely flight towards the carriers. On the outward journey the six TBFs had passed the ingoing Japanese bombers but, apart from a brief pass, the two sides ignored each other.

The Avengers were slightly ahead of the Marauders when the first sighting of the Japanese fleet was made. There was little time for them to drink in the sight of so many Japanese ships at one time before they were deploying for the attack itself. By the time Lieutenant Fieberling and his group had sighted the enemy, the Japanese had already had them under observation for five minutes. Extra fighters had been scrambled off the flight decks, within minutes those Zeros already in the air were swarming down astern of the slowly moving bombers, throttling back and firing quick sharp bursts into the pot-bellied Avengers, to which they could make but little reply.

Being the leading group, the Avengers drew the bulk of fighters down on their heads. A little way astern the Marauders led by Captain Collins watched as the six TBFs vanished in a cloud of Zeros. They could just make out the huge forms of aircraft-carriers surrounded by hordes of destroyers (or so it seemed to them) and Collins decided to work his way around and attack from their starboard bow. Before his big planes could complete this move another group of Zeros lashed down on them and they were soon in trouble. One, two, three, four, five splashes and fountains of spray marked the tombstones of Avengers; the cheering sailors and gunners aboard the warships kept score as if it was all a game. None of the TBFs got anywhere near close enough to make a decisive drop before they were skittled down.

The lone survivor of Fieberling's doomed squadron was that of Ensign Earnest. Already badly shot up, with the turret gunner killed, the hydraulic system shot away and controls badly damaged, this aircraft continued to bore in. The close-range guns of the fleet now opened fire and still Earnest kept coming. The elevator wires were shot away and great holes were punched through both wings. The Zeros pulled away leaving the Avenger to be finished off by the flak, but, with great skill, Earnest dropped at what he took to be a light cruiser and managed to keep his flying wreck in the air as he pulled away to the safety of the eastern horizon. He had no compass and, looking around, he could see none of his companions. Fortunately for him he could see no Japanese fighters either. The little Avenger limped away on her own towards Midway atoll. She made it.

Meanwhile the Marauders were the sole targets for the full, desperate fury of Nagumo's gunners. One of the twin-engined planes was heavily hit and cartwheeled into the ocean, its torpedo unlaunched. A second was shot through and through, but kept coming towards the *Akagi*, its large white Army Air Force star insignia plainly visible to the Japanese crew. It dropped its torpedo, which ran sluggishly wide of the mark, but the large aircraft itself seemed certain to crash into the flagship's bridge structure.

Still absorbing close-range fire it just missed *Akagi*, crossing from starboard to port and, as it did so, it burst into flames and crashed into the sea. The B-26 of Captain Collins continued its run, followed as closely as possible by that of Lieutenant Muri.

Both dropped at *Akagi* and kept going right over the big carrier. By the same combination of luck, skill and sheer audacity both aircraft got through, having been the closest men yet to the *Akagi* and lived to tell the tale. Muri headed back for Midway and made it, and Collins got his plane back as well. When they got back to Pearl Harbor the Army Air Force immediately went on the air to claim three direct torpedo hits on the enemy carriers. This story, being the first news that the American public received of the battle, received widespread publicity and was believed to be authentic. The navy had doubts about the claim but couldn't prove it. As a result the Army convinced most people it had won the Battle of Midway on its own. It was not until later that it was confirmed that there was not a single hit, not even one torpedo ran even near enough to be classed as a near-miss!

In the opinions of the watching experts aboard the Japanese warships the first attack had been uncoordinated and harmless, although none could deny the extreme gallantry of the airmen themselves.

Despite the fact that, out of ten aircraft, only three returned, and those in a badly damaged state, one of the Marauders crashed on landing at Midway, this brave attack had one outstanding result on the outcome of the battle. It convinced the wavering Nagumo that another air strike was necessary to obliterate the remains of any further Midway-based aircraft as suggested by Tomonaga a few minutes earlier. It was to prove a momentous decision.

And yet, when Nagumo issued his order at 0715, there was nothing to indicate that he had anything to fear other than repetitions, on a declining scale, of further shore-based attacks, and his fighters and gunners had demonstrated they were able to repel these with ease. So the order went out:

'Planes in second attack wave stand by to carry out attack today.'

To the waiting Kates on *Akagi* and *Kaga*, fitted with torpedoes ready to be used against ships, he ordered:

'Re-equip yourselves with bombs.'

On these two carriers the Kates began to be struck down on the lifts again and the laborious task of unshipping the torpedoes and rearming with heavy bombs began. Speed was of the essence and the cramped conditions below made the task a real chore. The efficient maintenance crews worked on in sweaty, but still cheerful, confidence.

However, barely had this arduous task been commenced when a startling message came from the seaplane reconnaissance of the cruiser *Tone*. This aircraft, it will be recalled, had been half an hour late in launching and now, at 0728, it relayed the following signal to *Akagi*:

'Ten ships, apparently enemy, sighted. Bearing 010°, distant 240 miles from Midway. Course 150°, speed more than 20 knots.'

This message must have struck Nagumo and his staff like a thunderbolt. Until then absolutely no indication had been received of any United States naval forces being at sea. The scout plane from *Chikuma* had covered that sector earlier without sighting anything at all.

Nagumo now found unpleasant alternatives piling up on him in rapid succession. He must strike at Midway which had shown itself remarkably resilient. But could he afford to ignore the American task force on his flank that was apparently closing fast? Further, before very much longer the returning aircraft from his first wave would be circling overhead and waiting to land, refuel and rearm. With his decks still cluttered with aircraft of the second wave, with half his bomber force rearming below decks, and with the need to fly off additional fighters to replace those just recently lost in combat, he had an unenviable choice to make.

But the report of the *Tone*'s aircraft had been frustratingly vague. No mention of aircraft-carriers had been made and if the enemy had only surface ships then he had sufficient time to recover his first wave, launch a second attack against Midway and then have his first wave standing by to attack the Americans. *If* it was only surface ships!

One thing was sure, that an answer would have to come quickly. The plotted position of the American ships was only 200 miles away, well within carrier-aircraft range. From the agitated bridge of the *Akagi* a curt signal went out to the search plane in effect telling him to do his job correctly.

For a time the rearming from torpedoes to bombs continued, but, at 0745, before any further news had been received from the *Tone* seaplane, Nagumo had a rapid change of heart. The change-over, already more than half complete, was halted. Those aircraft which still had torpedoes mounted were but half the normal torpedo-bomber force but that would, if it came to it, have to suffice.

Three minutes later the maddeningly vague seaplane made another report, which was no more illuminating than the first had been.

'Enemy ships have changed course to 080°.' Nothing more.

Back went a further rebuke, burning its angry way over the miles of ether from the worried admiral to his far-distant eye in the sky:

'Ascertain ship types and maintain contact.'

As if this was not sufficient, at 0800 came reports of further American air strikes coming in from the direction of Midway and most of the Japanese attention was forced to be concentrated on dealing with this more immediate threat.

This wave was the sixteen Dauntless dive-bombers led by Major Henderson. They approached at a height of 9000 feet in anticipation of their glide-bombing technique, which puzzled the watching Japanese below as being 'too high for torpedo-bombing and too low for dive-bombing.'

As before the ever-vigilant standing patrols of Zeros were soon streaking out to intercept. The Dauntless bombers appeared to the Japanese to be converging in two sections from the port and starboard bows. Unfortunately their timing was out and as a result each attack was dealt with individually, despite the initial surprise it had achieved.

The first group was led by Major Henderson himself but, well before they could get into position, they were under attack from the Zeros which swarmed up to meet them. The Dauntless bombers began to swoop down to 5000 feet and, like the torpedo-aircraft earlier, selected the *Akagi* as their target. But before they had covered half the distance they were caught in the same devastating cross-fire of machine-gun bullets and tracers and Major Henderson's aircraft was among the first to be destroyed; two others fell at the same time.

Captain Elmer G. Glidden took over command of the survivors and the second wave bore in. This group was taken under fire by the powerful anti-aircraft batteries of the battleship *Kirishima* who also loosed off several salvos from her main armament, no doubt using the splash-barrage technique to swamp the oncoming planes, although they were too high for this. Amazingly, the bombers survived all this heavy metal but, with outstanding courage, three of the Zero fighters sped into their own ships' barrage and on to the tails of the marine flyers. In seconds three Dauntless bombers had been sent flaming into the sea. The survivors pressed on in, this time heading for the *Hiryu*, and nine or ten managed to carry out very good attacks on that ship.

The Japanese carrier was surrounded by bomb bursts and hidden by towering walls of water and spray and, for a moment, it seemed as if she must have been badly hit. But within seconds she had emerged unscathed, her guns all firing flat out and none the worse for wear. Two more of these intrepid dive-bombers were shot down on their way out over the fleet and of the sixteen only half managed to return to Midway, six of them so badly shot about as to be write-offs. Lieutenant Daniel Iverson counted no less than 259 hits on his Dauntless and he himself had his throat microphone shot away although he suffered no injury. Alas, all their bravery and loss had accomplished nothing.

Nagumo had been startled by this attack, which had come so very close to destroying one of his carriers, at a time when he was preoccupied with the possibility of a major enemy force at his elbow. But he had little time to reflect on this fortunate survival before yet another part of the Midway strike force was overhead.

This time it was the mighty B-17s of Lieutenant Colonel Sweeney. Almost undetected by the Japanese force they maintained a stately and aloof position overhead at a height of 20,000 feet.

At such a height the Fortresses had nothing whatsoever to fear from the guns of the Japanese ships, and no Zeros were able to gain sufficient altitude in time to engage them either. Left completely unmolested the fourteen great bombers were able to make undisturbed target practice against the ships of their choice.

This time they chose the unfortunate *Hiryu* and her sister *Soryu*. The huge bomb doors swung open and from each B-17 8500lb of bombs dropped towards the scurrying targets far below. It was a very accurate and precise attack and again both carriers were deluged as huge columns of water reared up around them. But again both ships came through without a scratch or a casualty. Their bolts shot, the B-17s continued on their magnificent way and returned without loss to Midway. They at once issued claims to have scored direct hits on both carriers. 'Three flashes are seen on the two carriers, as white plumes of water rise all around them. Our planes rumble on and away, leaving one carrier smoking heavily', ran one highly colourful account of this action later. The *New York Times* screamed, in banner headlines: 'Army fliers blasted two fleets off Midway' and their journalist, Robert Trumbull, wrote that, 'army fliers who actually dropped the bombs hit three carriers, one cruiser and a battleship,' while General Hale claimed that the B-17s had won the battle on their own. All of which was of course complete and utter hogwash, but was believed by many people both at the time, and since.

So far torpedo-bombing, glide-bombing and altitude-bombing by shore-based aircraft had failed to score one single hit on Nagumo's force, but it was highly nerve-racking to have to undergo such concentrated attacks from a target all had thought would be something of a walk-over. And Midway Atoll had not yet finished.

Meanwhile, having survived everything thrown at him so far, Admiral Nagumo had also been cheered by a further report from the *Tone* seaplane which came in at 0809. The scout reported that:

'Enemy is composed of five cruisers and five destroyers.'

This was splendid news. Now all could continue to proceed as planned and there was still time to settle with Midway. A surface striking force consisting only of a cruiser squadron and destroyers would be easy meat for Nagumo to handle on his own, and at leisure. There was no need to call on the assistance of Yamamoto's battleships, or Kondo's. High optimism resumed on the bridge of the *Akagi*.

The dive-bombers of *Hiryu* and *Soryu* were ready for instant action, as were those Kates aboard *Akagi* and *Kaga* still armed with bombs. These could be launched against Midway, the returning first wave landed on, refuelled and rearmed and sent against the American cruisers.

So it was decided. But before this second revision could be implemented yet another range of American bombers was sighted bearing down on the fleet.

These were the eleven aged Vindicator dive-bombers of Major Norris, which had finally reached the fleet at their best speed. Although their planes were old, the crews were both well-trained in dive-bombing operations and determined to rectify, to the best of their ability, the so far lamentable score-sheet of their predecessors.

Once more though, the slow-moving bombers were set upon by such numbers of Zeros that Norris was forced to abandon his attack on the carriers. He turned to a nearer target, the battleship *Haruna* (which the Army Air Force had already claimed to have sunk some months before off Luzon in the Philippines!). Pushing over, most of the Vindicators followed him down towards this target at 0830. *Haruna* was firing with everything she had and the Zeros were still thick on their tails. Despite this the Vindicators pressed on in, spraying the upper-works of their giant adversary with machine-gun fire as they did so.

Again, sadly, all this display of heroism was not rewarded. Although many of the 500lb bombs were near misses the battle-ship was not even slightly damaged and two of the marine dive-bombers were shot down in flames. A couple of Vindicators did make a try for the *Akagi* but they were easily avoided and achieved nothing. Despite this, Norris and his men were more fortunate than most of his countrymen earlier that day, for nine Vindicators survived the Zeros and the flak to return to Midway. But even so it remained the hard, cold fact that once again, not a single scratch had been inflicted on the Japanese battle fleet and Midway was now left with nothing to throw at them.

Any fresh satisfaction that the Japanese may have felt about coming unscathed through this fourth major attack, had been nullified however by yet another message that had come in from *Tone*'s seaplane. This radio report was picked up at 0820 and, in yet another abrupt reversal of fate, it carried a message as worrying as it was unexpected:

'The enemy is accompanied by what appears to be a carrier.'

And as this grim news was being digested the rumble of depth-charges around the ships indicated that yet another facet of American defence preparations was in contact!

The American submarine *Nautilus* (Lieutenant Commander W. H. Brockman, Jr), had first picked up the PBYs' sighting reports of the Nagumo force that morning and she had been steering an interception course ever since.

Now the escorting Japanese destroyers had found her first, but the first attacks, at 0800, had been ineffective and had not deterred Brockman from pressing in still closer to seek a good target. In this he fared better than he had ever expected, for, when he raised his periscope at 0820, it was to find himself bang in the middle of the Nagumo task force and to see warships of all types, carriers, battleships, cruisers and destroyers, careering round in complicated circles with all guns firing flat out to engage the Vindicator dive-bombers swooping down on them.

In something of a classic understatement Brockman was to write in his combat report that,

'The picture presented on raising the periscope was one never experienced in peacetime practice.'

One can well believe it!

Even as he took an astonished look he was sighted, and, from close range, the battleship *Kirishima* was seen to train her entire starboard battery right at him and fire a broadside. Brockman could see emergency-turn flag signals being run up on the battleship's halyards and her searchlights began to lock right on to his periscope.

With considerable aplomb Brockman stayed long enough to fire a single torpedo right at his giant target before taking

Nautilus down quickly and deeply. The captain of the *Kirishima* was just as alert and swung his great ship round to avoid the attack. The range was 4000 yards and the torpedo passed astern. Diving down to 150 feet Brockman went to silent-running routine in readiness for the expected counter attacks.

These soon came and were intense in their nature. Depth-charge after depth-charge exploded close to the old boat rocking her about wildly. But she came through it all undamaged. By 0846 the attacks had died away and Brockman risked another look at the battlefield to see what was happening.

This time instead of a mad, rushing scramble of ships and blazing broadsides, all that met his eyes was an empty sea with just one lone destroyer left behind to keep him down as Nagumo's ships vanished over the horizon. At 0910 the skipper of the *Nautilus* was even bold enough to make an attack on this destroyer, the *Arashi*, the hunter stalked by the hunted, but he again missed. On his part Commander Watanabe of the *Arashi* made another attack on *Nautilus*, again without result, then sped off to catch up with the rest of the fleet.

Once more a seemingly ineffective, although equally bold and daring, attack was to lead to decisive result on the complex course of this fast-moving battle. The relatively minor pawn of the *Arashi* was another piece of the jigsaw that was beginning to fall into place.

While *Nautilus* and *Arashi* had been playing their own personal game of cat and mouse astern of Nagumo's carriers, further signals had been coming in to the *Akagi*'s crowded bridge. At 0830 the *Tone*'s seaplane had made another of the vague sighting reports that so characterised her unique brand of information that day. This one read:

'Two additional enemy ships, apparently cruisers, sighted. Bearing 008°, distant 250 miles from Midway. Course 150°, speed 20 knots.'

Although, again, it did not say much, the sighting of a second group of American warships showed Nagumo that his opponent's fleet was of considerable size, and, this being so, the odds must be that it contained at least one aircraft-carrier. It was therefore obvious that this carrier must have had ample time, since Nagumo's own force was first reported, to have prepared an air strike against him. That much was clear. If there was only one carrier then it was possible that they could ward off this attack, as they had those so far, and then turn and crush the American ship.

But even if this *was* the case, Nagumo was now in an even worse dilemma than before, because now the first of the returning first wave of aircraft from Midway were in sight and eager to alight on the decks of their carriers. And those decks were at that moment crammed with the aircraft of the second wave, armed with bombs and awaiting orders to hit Midway.

For the third time then, in what must have rapidly been assuming the worst hour of his life so far, Admiral Nagumo had to reverse his decision. Again his aircraft must prepare to attack ships and not the islands. Again his armourers must unclip the heavy bombs and replace the torpedoes. And this time it must be done with even more speed than before in order to get a striking force into the air against the enemy carrier.

But before this could be done his first wave had to be landed or else they would fall into the sea through lack of fuel. A crueller dilemma never faced any commander-in-chief than that faced by Nagumo at this time. Even as he struggled to make up his mind radio reports from some of his damaged first wave indicated that they would be lost if they could not land on immediately.

There were still the Val dive-bombers of *Hiryu* and *Soryu*, spotted and ready for action, which could be sent off right away against the American ships, but due to the need to fly off further fighter patrols, to take over from those already exhausted, there would be no opportunity to provide these Vals with any fighter protection of their own; and all aboard the Japanese fleet had just witnessed only too precisely what their fate would be if they went to the attack without such cover.

Likewise the Kates of the second wave spotted with their heavy bombs might not be so effective as with torpedoes but at least they might do some damage. But again the question of fighter cover remained the same.

In agony of spirit Nagumo made his final and most fateful decision. The Midway aircraft must be recovered first. To do this the existing aircraft lined up on deck must be struck down to clear the decks. Again the gongs shrilled out and down went the Kates for the third time that morning. Despite agitated signals from the *Hiryu*, sent over via the destroyer *Nowaki*, that an attack force of some kind be sent off immediately, Nagumo stuck to his guns. Soon the returning battle-scarred aircraft of Lieutenant Tomonaga began to drop down on to the welcoming flight decks of *Akagi* and *Kaga*, their pilots full of excited talk of damage inflicted on the enemy and of the remarkable success of Suganami's fighters in protecting the bombers.

Aboard the Japanese carriers worried eyes switched from the examination of watches and the bustling activity around the lifts to scan the eastern horizon with constant keenness. Would they be given the time?

Below decks all was confusion as the incoming waves were struck below, refuelled and rearmed, while the second wave was again brought up, armed with torpedoes and ranged yet again for their intended strike against the lone American carrier. The minutes crawled by and gradually the decks of both big carriers began to fill up. It looked as if they were going to make it.

Aboard the *Akagi* Commander Mitsuo Fuchida, who had been the original leader of the air strike force until struck down by an attack of appendicitis, was reduced to the rôle of helpless observer. It was a rôle that he did not enjoy and he was becoming almost frantic at the lack of action taking place on the *Hiryu* and *Soryu*, who were not affected by this complicated change-over to the same extent as were *Akagi* and *Kaga*.

The Nagumo force had turned to the north while these preparations were in force, in an attempt to throw any searching American striking force off the scent. It was at this time that Admiral Nagumo decided that his commanding officer, stolidly ploughing the seas many miles astern, ought to be informed of current developments and what his own intentions were to deal with them. Accordingly, at 0855, he signalled to Admiral Yamamoto:

'Enemy composed of one carrier, five cruisers and five destroyers sighted at 0800, bearing 010°, distant 240 miles from Midway. We will head for it.'

This signal, inaccurate as it is in its timings and omissions, has worried historians ever since. It is obviously a composite of all the various sightings received, although it omits the later additional ships spotted by *Tone*'s seaplane. Nonetheless it did convey to Yamamoto the fact that an American carrier was out, that Nagumo knew where it was, and that he intended to deal with it. Perhaps too much has been read into its faults, notably the fact that at the time it was sent Nagumo was withdrawing instead of 'heading for' the American fleet. However there is no doubt that, on conclusion of his complicated on-deck evolutions, Nagumo certainly had every intention of seeking his enemy and that is really all that matters.

Fuchida recorded his feelings at this vital moment:

'At least, I thought the dive-bombers group from *Hiryu* and *Soryu* was ready to attack the enemy, and I expected that it would be ordered off the carriers momentarily. This expectation, and hope, waned as the recovery of the first attack wave got under way with no sign that the dive-bombers had yet taken off.'

But Admiral Nagumo still hoped that he had the time to organise a concerted attack and not a piecemeal one. By 0918 the recovery of the last of the Midway strike force had been completed and the aircraft of that concerted wave were being ranged on deck. It was to consist of thirty-six Vals, fifty-four torpedo-equipped Kates, escorted by twelve Zero fighters which was all that could be made ready in time, three from each carrier of the force. Time of launch for this group was fixed at 1030.

While this feverish activity had been taking place *Tone*'s seaplane was running into difficulties. Despite the frustration her signals had caused there is no denying that, in finding the American task force, by shadowing it constantly and by sending in a stream of signals, she had given Nagumo a chance, more than an even break, at least so it seemed. Now she was at the limit of her endurance, had not been reinforced, and was fast running out of fuel. Her next message was received at 0847 and was as brief as her others had been. It simply stated: 'I am homeward bound.'

If her crew thought that they had done enough for one day

in escaping detection by the Americans they were in for a rude shock. Although Admiral Nagumo made no objection to her calling off her watch, her immediate CO, Rear Admiral Hiroaki Abe, was made of harder metal. The fate of one lonely seaplane from his own flagship was nothing when set against the Nagumo force as a whole. Sternly he instructed his young pilot:

'Postpone your homing. Maintain contact with enemy until arrival of four *Chikuma* planes. Go on the air with your long-wave transmitter.'

These latter had taken off to take up the screening of the American force but were not yet over their objective.

At 0918 Nagumo had swung his force round on course ENE and set speed at thirty knots to commence his attack.

But it was too late.

CHAPTER FOUR

THE GALLANT SACRIFICE

It will be recalled that, soon after the initial PBY sighting report
had come in, Fletcher had sent Spruance hurrying south-west
with task force 16 while *Yorktown* hung back to recover her
scouting planes. The time had been just after 0607 and Spruance
had lost no time in complying with his instructions.

The two carriers, with their escorting ring of six cruisers and
nine destroyers, had increased speed to twenty-five knots as they
pounded south-east through clear skies and moderate seas.
Their task was to close the 200-or-more-mile gap that lay
between them and the Japanese carriers as quickly as possible
so as to catch them in the midst of refuelling after the first strike
had returned.

It was necessary also to get within much shorter range of the
enemy to give his own aircraft the chance of reaching them,
attacking, and getting back. The maximum strike range of his
Devastator torpedo-planes was the vital factor here and that
was but 175 miles.

Spruance had calculated that he would reach this ideal flying-
off position by 0900, more than two and a half hours' steaming
away, but, as his force continued to run south-west, the ether
began to fill up with the reports of the Nagumo strike on Midway itself and of the heavy losses the defending aircraft had
taken. Hurried consultations took place which resulted in the
American admiral taking a decision as momentous as those
Nagumo was making that morning but, for him, with happier
consequences. The flying-off time for the initial American strike
was advanced by two hours and the risk was accepted that this
might prove fatal for many of the young airmen now awaiting
with considerable impatience the call to man their aircraft.

Accordingly task force 16 made preparations for launching and the two carriers separated from each other by several miles in order to facilitate the orderly forming up of their own strike squadrons prior to taking their departure for the target area.

The *Enterprise* took as her close escort the cruisers *Northampton*, *Vincennes* and *Pensacola* and the destroyers *Balch*, *Benham*, *Aylwin*, *Monaghan* and *Phelps*, while *Hornet* retained as her covering force the cruisers *Minneapolis*, *New Orleans* and *Atlanta*, with destroyers *Conyngham*, *Ellet*, *Worden* and *Maury*.

Launching commenced at 0702 and took an hour to complete as only half the strike force had been spotted on deck in readiness. This was due to the fact that a constant launch and recovery pattern had been maintained in order to keep a permanent eight-plane standing fighter patrol airborne over the force at all times.

The striking force was made up of thirty-five Dauntless dive-bombers from *VB-8* and *VS-8* with an escort of ten Wildcat fighters of *VF-8*, whose commanding officer, Lieutenant Commander Samuel G. Mitchell, was the overall fighter group commander also. The Dauntless bombers carried both 1000lb and 500lb bombs. *Hornet*'s final contribution was the fifteen Devastator torpedo-bombers of *VT-8* led by Lieutenant Commander John C. Waldron, whose skill, expertise and sometimes eccentric behaviour or methods of individual leadership, had already made him famous. These sixty *Hornet* aircraft were joined in the air by the *Enterprise* strike.

This consisted of thirty-seven Dauntless bombers of *VB-8* and *VS-8*, under Lieutenant Richard H. Best and Lieutenant Wilmer E. Gallaher respectively, together with the fourteen torpedo-bombers, also Devastators, of *VT-6* led by Lieutenant Commander Eugene E. Lindsey. Their fighter cover was in the form of ten more Wildcats, of *VF-6*, commanded by Lieutenant James S. Gray. Sixty-one aircraft in all. *Hornet*'s air group commander was Commander Stanhope C. Ring, while *Enterprise*'s group was led by Lieutenant Commander Clarence W. McClusky.

Even before the two American carriers were halfway through their launch programme, Spruance knew that he had been spotted and taken under constant observation of worrying persistency by a Japanese floatplane, but, despite the best efforts of his fighter patrols, this snooper continued its work unhampered.

The launch programme continued however, for Spruance knew well that the Japanese carriers would have to continue on their converging course long enough to recover their first strike. The possibility that a second strike could even now be airborne against him from these same aircraft-carriers seemed more than likely and it was with this fact in mind that the fighter escort for the outgoing American strike was so small, a total of twenty Wildcats in all. It was another calculated risk. It left the two American carriers with just thirty-six fighters of their own to defend them should Nagumo decide to strike at that time.

The thinking of the two opposing admirals on these points is fascinating. Nagumo declined to send in an early strike because of fear of heavy fighter defences to be overcome; Spruance sent his aircraft out with minimum defenders for fear of just such a strike. Had these been the only such vital decisions they might have cancelled each other out, but, as we know, they were not.

On completion of the launch the ships of task group 16 continued on their original course and maintained twenty-five knots.

Meanwhile the two striking forces moved out to the attack, but not, unfortunately, as a single combined group as planned. The sighting of the spotter plane convinced Spruance that all haste must be made to get in a decisive blow early. The dive-bombers of McClusky had been the first to take off as they had the greatest endurance. They could afford to circle using up fuel while the shorter-ranged Wildcats, and finally the Devastators, took off in their turn. Thus it was that the fighters were still flying off, and Waldron's Devastators were still revving up on *Hornet*'s after deck park, when McClusky was ordered to start off on his own and leave the others to catch up if they could.

McClusky's dive-bombers therefore took their departure just before 0800. Soon after, they were followed by the bombers of *Hornet* under Ring, with Commander Mitchell's Wildcat fighter group weaving above them.

Also airborne, and awaiting the launch of his own torpedo-bombers, was Lieutenant Gray with the *Enterprise* Wildcats. As they circled and waited for Lindsey's Devastators to form up they watched as Waldron took his torpedo-bombers off on their own, following a course well to the right of that taken by the fast-disappearing dive bomber groups. They too vanished to the south-west before Lindsey's final group set off in their wake. After a time however Lindsey's torpedo-bombers veered more to the left towards the departure route of the Dauntless bombers.

Keeping an eye on both groups of these slow-moving aircraft and, at the same time, constantly weaving to keep his faster Wildcats in touch with them, proved far from easy for Gray but for most of the outward flight he managed to keep them both in distant view.

Meanwhile Fletcher in the *Yorktown* had recovered his SBDs, flown off earlier, and made course to support Spruance, revving his ships up to a similar speed of twenty-five knots. Admiral Fletcher was still not totally convinced however that the Japanese carriers sighted so far were the only ones on the prowl to the west of him that morning. He still had an uneasy feeling that there might be more, as yet unreported, sneaking in for a surprise blow from the starboard beam.

His fears seem justified. It was known that the Japanese could muster at least eight carriers if they so wished. There was no reason why they should not have patched up both their Coral Sea casualties just as he had repaired his own flagship. Also the hazardous hit-and-miss reportings that had so marked that earlier conflict had stamped themselves on his mind. Caution was his watchword at this time.

Thus it was that not until half an hour after Spruance's attack groups had flown off to seek Nagumo did task force 17 start to launch her own striking force. Even then it was not every available bomber that Fletcher threw into the conflict; he quite deliberately kept back sufficient bombers to mount a second small strike should the occasion arise.

From *Yorktown*, at 0838, rose seventeen Dauntless dive-bombers led by Lieutenant Commander Maxwell F. Leslie, joined by Lieutenant Commander Lance E. Massey with twelve torpedo-bombers and covered by six Wildcats of Lieutenant

Commander John S. Thach's *VF-3. Yorktown*'s priority of launch also differed from *Hornet* and *Enterprise* in the fact that it was the Devastators of *VT-3* that were first off which were then instructed to head straight for the estimated enemy position.

Next up were the dive-bombers of *VB-3* and Leslie was instructed to circle for twelve minutes and then follow Massey's aircraft joining up en route to the target. Last up were the Wildcats of the escort and the last of these was not actually airborne until 0905.

Everything went without a hitch initially and within forty minutes the whole of the *Yorktown* assault force was in reasonable formation together, with the dive-bombers leading, followed by the Devastators down at 1500 feet, with the Wildcats stacked at two levels directly above them.

Behind them on the sunlit calm sea, *Yorktown* was busy ranging her second strike force in readiness for what the morning might bring.

Even as *Yorktown*'s air group was winging its way through the bright, calm morning, hardly disturbed by the faint breeze and odd patches of cloud, some 145 miles ahead of them the first of their comrades were going into action against the Nagumo task force. Over the horizon the peace and serenity of their departure was turning into a fire-streaked bloody hell in which the lives of the majority of gallant young men were to be snuffed out in a brief instant of glory.

On the decks of the four big Japanese carriers the organisation for the despatch of the now-readied striking force was proceeding with agonising slowness to the men waiting in anxiety. Then, at 0905, the first reports started to stream in from combat air patrols of a large number of carrier-type aircraft from the east rapidly closing. As these reports grew more numerous and the total number of incoming planes began to mount alarmingly, the admirals of the Japanese force knew at that instant that the trap they had so carefully laid had been sprung on themselves. For such numbers of planes could not come from one lone American carrier, but from two, three or God knew how many.

All thoughts about the required and ordered assembly of a complete air group now went by the board. From *Akagi* the signal went out to all carriers in company to speed all their preparations for take off. Far out ahead, on the carrier's starboard bow, just above the horizon the advance guard of the oncoming American air armada could be made out. They were low against the sun-drenched water – torpedo-bombers.

At once the whole weight of the standing air patrol, almost fifty Zero fighters, flung themselves against these planes. Like fifteen sparkling little toys the tiny distant shapes of the Devastators began to flame and burn, and then, one by one, cascade into the sea. It was Waldron's torpedo eight come to meet their destiny and gain their immortality.

But how was it that it was Waldron's squadron that appeared as the vanguard of the oncoming American hordes when they were the oldest and slowest aircraft in the assault force? Again fate had taken a hand.

It was Nagumo's 'run to the north' that led to this strange and tragic state of affairs. For by this manoeuvre the Japanese carriers evaded the whole Sunday-punch of the *Hornet*'s thirty-five Dauntless dive-bombers.

These, it will be recalled, had taken the direct course for the estimated position of the Japanese fleet. Had these ships maintained their original course, point of contact should have been reached by this powerful force some time between 0915 and 0930.

But, instead, the dive-bombers and fighters, led by Commander Ring, found only empty ocean. For a time Ring held his course in case the enemy carriers might have actually been some distance further to the south than originally plotted but, after several minutes, it became clear that this was not the case.

Commander Ring was therefore faced with a fifty-fifty chance. He could turn his whole force ninety degrees according to his hunches and search along the probable new course of the enemy, either north-west, away from Midway, or else south-east, towards that disputed island. Ring calculated that in order to recover his aircraft at the maximum speed Nagumo would have held on towards the atoll, embarking his returning bombers as he went. He guessed wrong.

Dipping over to port Ring led his combined force south-east, and away from the battle. As they held on their new course and the time passed with nothing to show for it but the barren ocean, *Hornet's* men knew they had failed. Soon, far away on the horizon, they saw the greasy black smoke of Midway's still-burning oil tanks. By this time several of the aircraft were running very low on fuel. Those that thought they could make it swung back to the north-east to gain the haven of their carrier. Thirteen of the SBDs were too low on fuel to even try; they settled for a landing on Midway itself, trusting that this was still a practical proposition. Eleven made it and two ended up in deep waters of the lagoon. As for the rest of the group, the twenty Dauntless bombers made it back finally to *Hornet* and landed on, but every one of Mitchell's ten Wildcat fighters ran out of fuel before they could gain that safety and all had to ditch in the sea.

Of the eleven bombers which made it down safely on Midway all were refuelled as quickly as the hand methods the Japanese had left them with would allow and they got back into the air again, determined to somehow get back into the scrap. But they never did. It was late afternoon when they finally returned to *Hornet*, dispirited and weary.

The same decision that had beaten Ring had to be faced a little while later by McClusky leading the *Enterprise* dive-bombers. Again only empty sea met his gaze at the estimated point of contact. What to do? Again, like Ring, he held his course for a short while without reward. His guess was sweep to the north-west. The thirty-seven little dive-bombers came round on the new bearing. The time was 0935.

This left Waldron's low-flying TBDs to face the music alone for when, some considerable time after the SBDs had reached the same point, torpedo eight reached the enemy's estimated location Waldron did not hold on but immediately came right and bore in towards the true position of the Japanese fleet. His decision was absolutely correct and made in an instant. He and his squadron paid for his intelligence with their lives, almost to a man.

It seemed that Waldron was also intelligent enough to realise that in an attack such as the one contemplated, an all-out assault against a more powerful and a forewarned enemy, his lumbering torpedo-bombers would stand little or no chance of coming out alive.

On the back of his final attack plan Waldron had written his message to his squadron:

'I feel we are ready . . . ' he wrote, adding prophetically: 'If there is only one plane left to make a final run in, I want that man to go in and get a hit. May God be with us all.'

He also showed a similar awareness, even resignation to his probable fate, at his final briefing session with Captain Mitscher of the *Hornet*, just before his last take-off. He promised Mitscher that, no matter what, he would press home his attack even if there was absolutely no chance of getting back to his ship.

En route, Waldron's squadron had lost contact with Mitchell and Ring but this made no difference either. At 0925 the Japanese fleet was in sight. The Zeros fell out of the sky like a flight of silver wasps, machine-guns chattering and snarling, three Japanese fighters for each Devastator. It was a massacre. Waldron wiggled his wings and put the nose of his aircraft down. His fourteen compatriots did likewise. They still had eight miles to go towards the Japanese carriers when the first flak also started bursting around them, but by that time the fourteen had become ten.

Still the survivors held grimly on while their aircraft were torn to shreds around them. Five minutes to go to release and the ten had become five. Waldron's voice was heard over the airwaves in those incredible final seconds.

'How am I doing . . . Attack immediately . . . My two wingmen are going into the water . . . '

Then the Zeros cut short his words. His aircraft was hit in its fuel tanks and burst into flames before cartwheeling into the water. Within seconds the surviving three on his heels had been torn apart also. Just one Devastator continued to bore in, shreds of fabric flying from its chewed-up wings.

This last torpedo-bomber of the doomed torpedo eight was piloted by Ensign George Gay. His was the rear plane of the formation and he watched in horror as each of his friends and companions died in brief succession.

He recalled Waldron's final request: 'If there is only one plane left . . . ' Well – that was him.

Through the flak he could see the shapes of the speeding destroyers of the screen, hulls punctuated by flaming guns, all concentrating on him personally. Astern he heard his gunner cry out as Zero bullets smashed into his body.

Still he flew in and now he could see in the distance the huge form of a Japanese carrier. He pushed his torpedo release button hard but nothing happened. At once he jerked with all his strength at the manual release and his torpedo dropped away. Like all the others released by torpedo eight it was a miss.

His riddled aircraft staggered on over the bow of his target and then flopped heavily into the water. Gay opened the cockpit canopy and swam away as best he could as the Devastator sank beneath the waves taking his dead gunner with it. Luckily the inflatable life-raft floated free of the wreckage and Gay managed to crawl inside it to dubious safety. He covered his head to avoid being spotted from the air. But he need not have worried, the Japanese were fully occupied. Thus passed *Hornet*'s gallant *VT-8*. Of fifteen aircraft and thirty men Gay was the only survivor.

On the Japanese flagship the word that the whole attacking force had been destroyed was received with jubilation. These aircraft had been identified as carrier-based aircraft and, as such, they were the most dreaded of their opponents to date. Now all fifteen had fallen in as many minutes and not one of their torpedoes had struck any ship of the Nagumo force. But the Japanese fighters were given no chance for any self-congratulation for, even as the last aircraft of *VT-8* smashed into the sea, a fresh wave of American torpedo-bombers was observed, boring in with equal determination.

At this time the formation of the Nagumo force was still holding up well to the attacks. The four carriers were placed centrally, in box formation initially, while on their original course of 140°. The *Hiryu* was leading the port column, with *Soryu* some 4000 yards astern of her. Some 1500 yards away the other side of the defensive cruising box was led by the flagship, *Akagi*, with *Kaga* astern at the same distance as *Soryu*. Ahead and between these first carriers was the battleship *Kirishima*, while in a similar position, between the two carrier columns, but slightly astern, was the second powerful battleship of the force, *Haruna*. Thus positioned, both capital ships were well placed to contribute heavy covering flak from their massive AA batteries against attacks directed at, or along, the line of advance. This was the natural line of approach for dive-bombers as it presented the whole length of the carrier's flight-deck as an aiming point.

The cruisers appear to have been placed slightly away from this inner group, to port and to starboard, while the light cruiser *Nagara* acted as 'guide to the fleet' from ahead of *Kirishima*, and had her ten screening destroyers placed ahead and on the flanks of the formation. One of these was, of course, missing from her place on the screen, the *Arashi* who, after her hunt for *Nautilus*, had cracked on speed to rejoin from astern, but she had not yet caught up.

This formation had given way to a similar one at 0917, when Nagumo had led round on his new course of 70°, and then, 30°, but the relative positions of the ships remained generally the same. However under the impetus of the mounting scale of blows now aimed at them, the precise positioning of the ships was becoming a little ragged.

Thus it was that Lindsey found them at 0930.

Lieutenant Commander Eugene E. Lindsey had taken his strike off on a course described as slightly diverging from that flown by the Devastator bombers of Waldron's group; nonetheless Lieutenant James S. Gray, with his small force of Wildcats flying top cover for both groups, later stated that this was not excessive. Lindsey had arranged that, at the commencement of his attack, he would signal Gray to bring his fighters down to cover their tails, but until then they should maintain the necessary altitude required to give them a chance against the deadly Zeros.

Gray, accordingly, kept to this plan, but, during the outward flight, had been forced by the spreading out of both groups under his charge, into a position whereby he lost touch with them.

The Wildcats nevertheless stuck to the original scheme and circled over the Japanese fleet, awaiting Lindsey's signal to announce he was ready to go in. But this signal never came. Even as Gray circled, the fourteen Devastator torpedo-bombers were feathering the waves and deploying for action.

Whereas Waldron's group had enjoyed a few fleeting moments of immunity, due to their catching the Japanese by surprise, Lindsey's airmen found the enemy both alert and already deploying in a defensive swing away from his position of attack. Even before the escorting Japanese fighters started to slash down towards them the Devastator bombers of the *Enterprise* group had lost valuable moments by being forced to circle around to get into fresh attack positions against the violently swerving Japanese carriers.

Nonetheless Lindsey managed to make his alignment on the *Akagi* and to order the attack to be pressed home. By that time many of the Zero fighters, already low over the water after finishing off Waldron, were in among the slow-moving torpedo-planes and this second band of brave men began to be mercilessly cut to pieces.

From *Akagi* it appeared that Lindsey's force had split into two wedges which were attempting to make a concerted attack from either bow, from 30° to starboard and 40° to port respectively. They approached in single columns and were within five miles of the ships when they were first intercepted.

The destroyer screen was firing by this time but once more it was the protecting Zeros which inflicted the carnage. One by one the Devastators flamed, crumpled and skidded into the sea at over one hundred miles an hour, the impact smashing planes, crew and torpedoes into fragments. A few exploded in the air just above the sea, which quickly sucked the wreckage under the waves.

Again the watching sailors and gunners aboard the Japanese fleet were treated to a grandstand view of the slaughter. The numbing fear in each man's throat at the sight of so many deadly torpedo-carriers approaching was quickly replaced by a mixture of relief and awe as the TBDs toppled like crazy tops into the ocean. The Japanese crews shouted, whistled and cheered, according to one eyewitness as the deadly score mounted up.

Only about seven TBDs eventually reached the torpedo-release point against *Akagi* and, to her watching crew, it seemed that they might be in danger. But, to their surprise, no drops were made at this target. Instead the survivors switched to the *Hiryu*, to port and astern of the flagship at this moment.

Fuchida later described the final seconds of this very brave attack:

'Seven enemy planes finally succeeded in launching their torpedoes at *Hiryu*, five from her starboard side and two from port. Our Zeros tenaciously pursued the retiring attackers as far as they could. *Hiryu* turned sharply to starboard to evade the torpedoes, and we watched anxiously to see if they would find their mark. A deep sigh of relief went up when no explosion occurred, and *Hiryu* soon turned her head to port and resumed her original course.'

Of the fourteen Devastators that followed Lindsey in that last headlong charge, only four survived to limp home to the *Enterprise*, and Lieutenant Commander Lindsey was not one of the survivors.

Hardly had this second massacre taken place than the excited Japanese lookouts spotted yet another wave of torpedo-bombers approaching. Would it never end? Again tired gunners tracked round and weary ammunition parties brought up fresh shells. The Zero fighters, already having chalked up a performance unequalled in efficiency of fleet defence this day, swung around to intercept this new threat. For the more perceptive of the watching officers aboard the carriers there was the nagging fear that, if this kept up at such a pace, the Japanese defences, no matter how brilliantly they were operating, must surely be swamped.

The newcomers to this field of carnage were *Yorktown*'s groups. Although launched way behind the others they had nevertheless arrived on the scene of battle at an opportune moment, had they then had the opportunity to co-ordinate their attacks. Alas Lieutenant Commander Lance E. Massey, with his twelve Devastators of *VT-3*, although in company with both his fighter escort and dive-bomber group at the moment of the sighting of the Japanese fleet, was to have no better fortune.

As the *Yorktown* group deployed it was seen that the earlier, rigidly formal layout of Nagumo's force was now sadly in disarray. Not surprisingly the frantic swerving and high-speed diversionary tactics of the carriers, under torpedo-bomber assault, had left the fleet fragmented into isolated groups, all trying to conform to a general line of advance but, in essence, presenting no discernible pattern to the American airmen as they made their approach.

By breaking up the defensive pattern of fire this was a bonus for Massey but, on the other hand, it made the careful selection of the most suitable target, and the steady approach course required to pin it down, an even more difficult undertaking.

The attack of Massey's torpedo-bombers showed every promise of being the first co-ordinated attack the Americans had been able to launch that day, for the seventeen dive-bombers of Lieutenant Commander Maxwell F. Leslie's group were in company, as were the six Wildcats of Lieutenant Commander Thach.

Yorktown's groups had been following the same general flight pattern as Waldron but further to the north, therefore they were not quite so much thrown out by the northern course diversion that had split up both *Enterprise* and *Hornet*'s air groups. Even so, when first sighted, the whole madly careering bunch of Nagumo's warships were between thirty and forty miles off the Americans' starboard beam. Veering hard right the three components of *Yorktown*'s striking force prepared for a classic combined assault.

As they did so they hit cloud and at once the whole carefully rehearsed plan was ruined. Leslie's dive-bombers climbed above it, to gain the necessary height for their assault, but, in doing so, they lost radio contact with Massey's torpedo-bombers. These, in turn, were dropping down to sea level and aligning themselves with the carriers ahead. For the first time the comforting sight of Thach's six Wildcats, above and astern, gave the torpedo-bomber pilots some reassurance about their sterns, leaving them to concentrate on a good approach pattern.

It will be noted, from Fuchida's quoted extract earlier, that he has combined, in his account, both the attacks of Lindsey and the attack of Massey as one concentrated assault. But in fact the two attacks were separated by almost half an hour in commencement, although running into each other in combat. Thus it was just on 1000 that Massey's Devastators followed the well beaten path in towards *Akagi* and her sisters.

The decks of the Japanese carriers were alive with the returning fighters of their combat air patrols. Although few had, as yet, run out of fuel during their defensive missions, a number had exhausted their ammunition in destroying the earlier assaults. These put down and were quickly rearmed and then cheered along the flight-decks as they hurtled off to re-engage. And there was need for them this time, because of the new factor of the Wildcat fighters making their first appearance on the scene.

This gave the Japanese some conception of just how close the two carrier fleets had drawn to each other now, if the single-engined, short-range Wildcats were about, then the striking force from the four big Japanese carriers should have no difficulty in finding their opponents.

By the time the American aircraft had covered about half the distance to their targets from their deployment zone they had run into that imposing wall of Zero fighters. The six Wildcats had little opportunity to give their protection to the torpedo bombers, for they were smothered in defending fighters. The Zeros were now at the peak of their form, having been fighting for over an hour against not very strong opposition. Outflown and outnumbered, Thach and his little band were soon fighting desperately for their own lives in the midst of this swirling dog-fight. The first Wildcat began its long dive towards the sea, trailing smoke and flame. Far below them another grim slaughter was already well under way. Of the dive-bombers there was no sign at all.

Between the milling fighters and the Devastators below, the sky was filling up with more Zeros, and, before the torpedo-bombers had reached their final run-in positions their ranks had been seriously depleted. Seven of the twelve Devastators made it this far; behind them the broken machines of their comrades burned and sizzled on the wreckage-strewn water.

Of these seven, two more, including Massey himself, blew up under murderous fire. The remaining five, in two small groups, split their attacks between two of the carriers, the *Kaga* and the *Hiryu*, and managed to launch their torpedoes. But harassed as they were by flak and fighters, with their targets swirling out of their sights under full helm, their missiles, not surprisingly, also ran harmlessly clear, and two more Devastators paid the inevitable price as they struggled to get clear. Another blew up as it crossed the far screen. Of *VT-3*'s twelve aircraft which had commenced the attack at 1000 only two survived to make their way silently back to the *Yorktown* at 1020.

So far the attempts by the American carriers to intervene in the battle had been even less successful than those of the shore-based aircraft. Forty-one torpedo-bombers had made the attempt, only six had survived. A crushing blow had been parried with relative ease and full credit for this convincing example of aerial defence should go to the defending Zeros, whose performance up to that moment had just about reached its peak in efficiency.

Not a single torpedo had come anywhere near its target in return for this gallant sacrifice. It is said that when Winston Churchill was told the details of their heavy losses later, he wept.

And yet all their sacrifices were *not* in vain. The valour and determination of these young men, although seemingly rewarded solely by their own deaths, was yet another facet of this battle that was to lead to almost instant retribution. By bringing down on their own heads the whole wrath of the defending fighters, by forcing the tight defensive cordon of the Japanese fleet to become split up into a disorganised rabble, even though for only a few moments, the torpedo-bomber crews achieved far more than they knew. The Nagumo force had forgotten to look upward.

Even now, after the passage of over thirty years, this fact seems inexplicable. All the other errors committed this day can be understood, explained and certainly sympathised with, but the failure of this crack force, which was the leading exponent of dive-bombing (and the most successful exponent of that method of attack ever seen), to have overlooked that most obvious of facts, that where there were carrier-based torpedo-bombers and fighters there must, inevitably, be the longer-ranged dive-bombers also, is just inexplicable.

It is true that the Japanese were denied the overwhelming advantage of radar. They had to rely on eyesight only for news and identification on the incoming air raids which only gave them a few minutes warning of each attack. Conversely the American task groups would have at least twenty minutes fore-knowledge of every Japanese raid, and could tell its size, course and speed.

But, even allowing that this made a colossal difference, the surprise the Americans had achieved had already been lost by the arrival of the slowest aircraft first. The Japanese must have realised that the torpedo-bombers would not attack alone as this was against every known rule of carrier warfare. If the dive-bombers had not shown up it must surely have been obvious that they were not far away. If not, then they would also be up high, ready to commence their screaming, precision dives. Why then had the air controllers of the defending fighters allowed each one of their fighters to be drawn down to sea level in this manner, leaving the skies above the fleet empty?

The comment on this aspect of their defence work that is quoted by Morison in his work, that: 'There is a marked tendency for our fighters to over-concentrate on enemy torpedo planes,' is not satisfactory on its own.

Of course the fighters, meeting wave after wave of attackers, scoring victory after victory, would be drawn, like bees to a honeypot, to the low-flying torpedo-bombers, but that is precisely what the air controllers were there for, to anticipate the mistakes of the pilots and look out for the less immediate and developing facets of the battle. No pilot, with his limited range of vision, could do this, he could only look for the nearest enemy aircraft and engage it. It was the duty of the controllers to ensure that an adequate number of fighters were deliberately held back from combat to ensure that there was a reserve for the unexpected.

On this day it was not done. Perhaps in the heat of this rapidly developing battle there are many reasons why not.

The splitting up of the force, while taking avoiding action, would tend to lead each controller aboard each of the four carriers to, quite naturally, pull in his own fighter aircraft to protect his own ship. To each observer it is one's own vessel that seems the focal point of each assault and there may have been a tendency to leave alternative cover to 'the other three', while they fought off their own attackers. As each carrier interpreted this in the same way, all the fighters were brought down.

Then again there was the limiting need of each carrier to keep enough fighters on hand to launch with the planned counter-blow against the American ships. By this time, 1025, Admiral Nagumo had already signalled that each carrier was to launch her strike force when ready, and indeed the first Zeros of the attacking formations were already beginning to speed down the flight decks. Only those fighters already committed to the defence of the fleet were not involved and these were on the wave crests, another reason for none being up above the clouds on the alert.

On all the Japanese carriers now, the decks were humming with the roars of motors as the aircraft of the strike waves prepared for take-off. For most of the morning the Nagumo force had undergone wave after wave of the heaviest air attacks ever directed against it, and it had withstood them all, altitude-bombing, torpedo-bombing, glide-bombing, dive-bombing, even strafing from the odd fighter, with complete success. Ninety-two American aircraft had attacked, no hits had been made and only thirty-seven aircraft had survived. Now, at last, within three minutes the mighty fist of the Nagumo force would stretch out, as so often before, and crush for ever the American fleet which dared to stand up to it in this unprecedented manner.

It was 1027.

CHAPTER FIVE

THE MOMENT OF TRUTH

Although the American carrier aircraft had been in contact with Nagumo's carriers for more than an hour, it was not until 1000 that any member of the various groups involved had signalled the fact that they had actually *found* the enemy to their commanders back at the two American task groups. Thus the period of agonised waiting that both Rear Admirals Spruance and Fletcher had undergone since the departure of their airmen was becoming almost unbearable.

Perhaps then Fletcher's fears that the wily Japanese had the bulk of their carriers swinging in behind the American ships, ships left almost naked now of air cover were justified. Who could tell?

Lieutenant Gray, it will be remembered, was circling above the Japanese fleet awaiting his call from the torpedo-bombers which never came. For forty minutes he continued his lonely patrol thus, above the cloud formations which effectively screened from him the carnage going on below. No other American formation came into sight and no patrolling Zeros disturbed his solitude. At the end of this time his Wildcats, having achieved absolutely nothing, were beginning to get low on fuel.

At 0952, therefore, he broke his wireless silence to convey this fact to McClusky, whom he had not seen since take-off. Eight minutes later he followed this up with a sighting report and *this* was the first information that Fletcher and Spruance had that they had guessed right after all.

Meanwhile Leslie was also cursed with incredible bad fortune. Soon after his dive-bomber force had taken departure from the American fleet Leslie had commenced a routine check-out of the new electrical bomb-release gear that had been fitted to his Dauntless bombers only recently. No American bomber took off from its carrier's vulnerable wooden flight-deck with a 500lb or 1000lb bomb slung beneath, fully armed. Instead, once safely aloft and clear of the ship, the pilot armed the bomb by cocking a trigger mechanism, which would ensure detonation on contact, hopefully, with the target.

But, when Leslie himself used the new electrical switch to carry out this operation, his 1000lb bomb was released and fell harmlessly into the Pacific. At first he did not realise what had happened but frantic signals from his wingman eventually confirmed his worst fears. He was going into the most important battle of his life without his bomb load!

Nor was that the end of the matter, for three other Dauntless bombers were found to have suffered the same fate. At once the group's striking power was reduced by almost a quarter.

Silently cursing his bitter fate Leslie determined that, despite this, he would lead his group into the attack in order to maintain good control. He would have to do the best he could with his machine-guns and offer himself as an alternative target. This way at least the attack would not lose cohesion through loss of its leader and the thirteen remaining aircraft could arm manually and follow him in as planned. They flew on south-west.

At 1020 and at a height of 20,000 feet he sighted smoke to his right and knew he had made it. The seventeen dive-bombers tipped over on their right wings and came round in a sweeping curve and they were soon able to make out a large number of Japanese warships manoeuvring at high speeds and throwing off a stream of flak.

Soon Leslie could make out the long-sought shapes of the great wide wooden deck of a carrier which appeared to have just turned a full 180° and the broad semi-circle left by her wake was clearly visible. To Leslie and his pilots she looked enormous and he had no hesitation in selecting her as his target. This ship would seem to have been the *Kaga*.

Meanwhile McClusky was casting northward seeking Nagumo. He was rewarded, at 0955, with the sight of a long, white wake in the water below, crossing his own north-westerly course on a north-easterly bearing. It was obviously made by a high-speed craft, certainly a destroyer therefore, making up lost ground to rejoin the main fleet, or so McClusky reasoned. It was indeed so, for the vessel below him, digging in her stem and tucking down her stern at thirty-three knots, and throwing spray back over her fo'c'sle in her eagerness to get back into the fight, was none other than the destroyer *Arashi*. Commander Watanabe, having given up his abortive hunt for the *Nautilus*, was now anxious to rejoin his flotilla and add the weight of his own ship's gunfire to the anti-aircraft defences of the fleet. Unwittingly he laid a perfect trail for the thirty-seven dive-bombers of McClusky's force.

Within minutes McClusky was over the Japanese fleet, approaching from the south-west, while Leslie's Dauntless force was approaching from the south-east. As both dive-bomber groups took sight of their enemy the final dying kicks of the torpedo-bomber assaults were being snuffed out and the ships presented a highly disordered picture to the American dive-bomber pilots.

McClusky identified his targets as the *Akagi* and *Kaga*, the two largest vessels, and a dispute has continued ever since about which ships were attacked by which aircraft. Although this will now never be firmly established beyond all doubt it now seems much more likely that the ships that the *Enterprise* SDBs actually turned on to at 1020 that morning were the *Soryu* and the *Akagi*. These two carriers seem to have executed an emergency turn, just prior to the final attack, which brought them both round on to a southerly course, *Akagi* turning to port and taking the lead on this new bearing, and the smaller *Soryu* turning to starboard and coming up astern in reverse order to the original line of advance. *Kaga* had similarly turned a full circle to starboard but maintained her position, thus placing her to the east of the *Akagi* and *Soryu* but on the same course and thus she was the vessel that Leslie and his aircrew latched on to first.

The *Hiryu* had not turned with the other carriers at this time and this placed her well to the north of their position and steaming on an opposite course to the other three Japanese carriers. This led to her escape from detection and attack at this time and cloud cover continued to shield her during the cataclysmic

8 113

TAKASU
4 BATTLESHIPS
2 CRUISERS
12 DESTROYERS

YAMAMOTO
3 BATTLESHIPS
1 CARRIER
1 CRUISER
9 DESTROYERS

KONDO
2 BATTLESHIPS
1 CARRIER
5 CRUISERS
8 DESTROYERS

TANAKA
CONVOY
1 CRUISER
8 DESTROYERS

KURITA
4 CRUISERS
2 DESTROYERS

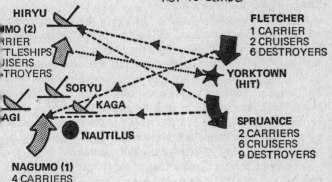

MIDWAY 2

EXCHANGE OF CARRIER
STRIKES – 4 JAPANESE
CARRIERS DESTROYED –
1 US CARRIER DAMAGED
JAP SURFACE FORCES CLOSE

NOT TO SCALE

HIRYU

[NAGU]MO (2)
[CAR]RIER
[BAT]TLESHIPS
[CRU]ISERS
[DES]TROYERS

SORYU

KAGA

[AK]AGI

NAUTILUS

FLETCHER
1 CARRIER
2 CRUISERS
6 DESTROYERS

**YORKTOWN
(HIT)**

SPRUANCE
2 CARRIERS
6 CRUISERS
9 DESTROYERS

NAGUMO (1)
4 CARRIERS
2 BATTLESHIPS
3 CRUISERS
11 DESTROYERS

MIDWAY

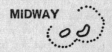

events which now befell her sisters.

On sighting the two carriers wide open for attack, and thus being afforded an instant affirmation of his good judgement, McClusky continued to act coolly and rationally. He had under his command two squadrons, Lieutenant Richard Best's *VB-6*, and Lieutenant Gallaher's *VS-6*.

VS-6's Dauntless dive-bombers had been the first squadron off the *Enterprise* flight-deck, and had to circle while the others took off and formed up also; because of this they were armed with only 500lb bombs. Gallaher's aircraft were sent against the smaller target, the *Soryu*, but only by chance, while Best, with his Dauntless bombers carrying the much more lethal 1000lb bomb loads, was sent in against the *Akagi*. However as three of the dive-bombers from *VB-6* went for the wrong target in error, the end result was, as Professor Morison states succinctly, '... each carrier got its share of the half-ton bombs.'

On receipt of their orders both these squadrons made 70° turns at just over 280 mph to get in position and then split into their respective groups and commenced their dives. There was no interference from any Japanese fighter during this operation, and the anti-aircraft fire was sparse and relatively ineffective.

In truth the Japanese were taken completely by surprise.

The bare bones of the Japanese log conveys with just what speed the fatal part of the battle was decided.

0722 (Tokyo time): '*Akagi* sees *Kaga* being dive-bombed.'
0725: '*Akagi* notes fires on *Kaga*.'
0726: 'Three bombers dive on *Akagi* ... '

Thus it was that Leslie's group struck just four minutes ahead of Best and Gallaher.

Aboard the carriers themselves all was tense and calm with the launch of the first wave of the air striking force only minutes away. Visibility was described as good, although there were cloud formations up at 3000 feet with breaks. These, it was thought, would give the Japanese carriers good cover for any further searching American aircraft. In fact they did the reverse and hid the oncoming dive-bombers until the last possible moment.

At 14,500 feet above the basking task force Leslie was grouping his team for the final assault. His target was described as ' . . . one of the biggest damn things . . . ' ever seen and there can be little doubt she was the *Kaga*. Minus his bomb Leslie pushed over, and, at just under 300 mph, hurtled down through the gap in the clouds; behind him the rest of his squadron followed.

As they closed on their target sporadic flak started to pepper the sky but there was no staying their onward approach. The great red disc painted on *Kaga*'s broad flight deck grew ever-larger in Leslie's sights. Her deck was crowded with aircraft, most with their propellers already turning, a Zero was racing along the deck in a vain attempt to beat the inevitable.

Powerless to hurt this huge monster himself, Leslie nonetheless vented his wrath by firing at the aircraft and bridge structure with his machine-guns as he swooped low across his target at 4000 feet. Then his guns jammed on him. His number two, Lieutenant Holmberg, pressed on in closer, for he was carrying his 1000lb bomb and meant to make it count. It did. At 2500 feet he released and soared away into the sky.

Behind him roared the other dive-bombers, three waves in all, approaching the *Kaga* from the starboard bow, starboard quarter and port quarter respectively, thus effectively splitting the already dazed and unprepared gunners. Most of the bombers released at 2500 feet and most were either on target or not very far off it.

Within seconds the proud carrier was a blazing wreck.

The first bombs that struck hit her wooden flight-deck forward, just in front of the island superstructure. The blast and fragments of this explosion completely destroyed this section, the heart of the ship, killing her captain and turning the command post into a charnel house of dead and maimed men. An aviation fuel bowser had been located just by this spot and it ignited in a shock-wave of flame and smoke, the fires running across the flight deck in blazing rivulets.

Command of the stricken vessel was assumed by Commander Amagai but there was little he could do to save the ship for she had already been struck by a further three heavy bombs.

One by one they crashed into the carrier's decks. Forward, centre and aft, the *Kaga* was sewn up by Leslie's team as neatly as could be. Each successive blast ripped open a further section of her deck, gouged through into the hangars below filled with refuelling and rearming aircraft, and exploded in a series of mighty convulsions that shook and disembowelled the ship. Blazing fuel from the pulverised aircraft ignited and joined with the fires from the explosions. Fire-fighting and rescue teams hurrying to one blast area were annihilated by the next hit and soon the fires were raging uncontrollably. The *Kaga*'s innards were strewn with piles of mutilated and burning corpses. Within minutes the main magazines began to blow up as warheads detonated with the heat.

Despite the fact that she took four direct hits and was little more than a burning, gutted hulk, strewn with dead and dying men, the *Kaga* remained afloat. Many of her crew had already given her up for lost and had taken to the water.

For more than three hours some of the survivors gallantly attempted to fight the colossal fires but it was useless and Amagai, after being trapped by a sea of flames on the ship's starboard boat deck, gave the order to abandon ship. By this time the heat was detonating the ammunition in the anti-aircraft guns and the paintwork was now on fire on the remaining superstructure.

The two destroyers left behind to tend to her, *Hagikaze* and *Maikaze*, manoeuvred around, powerless to do anything except pick up blackened and burnt men from the water, as the fierceness of the fires prevented them from positioning themselves alongside to embark the survivors still on board.

Amagai did manage to get back on board once during a lull in the fires, but had to rapidly leave again when they broke out with renewed violence. The end for the *Kaga* came at 1925, nine hours after taking her supreme punishment, when her hull was riven by two gigantic internal explosions. The fire and flames leapt up higher than ever, before the black and twisted hulk finally went down in a cascade of steam and smoke. Into the depths of the Pacific, the bottom hereabouts is over 2500 fathoms, the *Kaga* took with her more than 800 members of her crew and aircrew and almost every one of her aircraft. Not one of Leslie's aircraft had been hit.

The *Akagi* had fared no better.

Lieutenant Best's team, less three aircraft which followed Gallaher, commenced their dives on Nagumo's flagship some minutes after Leslie's team had scored their first hit. The *Akagi* had about two-score aircraft ranged on deck at this time. The first bomb detonated in the water close alongside the bridge structure and seconds later the first hit was made.

This bomb, which proved to be the fatal injury, hit the amidships lift, punching through it to explode in the hangar below packed with aircraft and strewn with bombs and torpedoes, which had not been stowed away due to the haste caused by the continual changes in the rearmament of the planes. Again warheads ignited and the fuel tanks of the aircraft burst into sheets of flame, cremating hangar crew and fire-fighting teams alike. Thick clouds of choking black smoke poured through the bowels of the stricken vessel overcoming many crew members.

A second direct hit was made almost immediately on the port side of the flight deck aft. This explosion again caused the immediate detonation of the bombs, torpedoes and aviation fuel of the packed aircraft there, whirling shattered aircraft into the air and over the side, and sweeping away the armourers and flight deck personnel like blazing leaves in a bonfire. The fires then rapidly spread to engulf the whole of the stern of the ship, and many of the Japanese pilots and aircrews were burnt alive in their stationary planes. The whole flight deck abaft the bridge became a vast funeral pyre for these, the cream of the Japanese Navy flyers. The blazing pall of smoke bore a resemblance to the fiery pall that had covered the battleship *Arizona* at Pearl Harbor; never had vengeance come so violently and so precisely from out of the sky.

As explosion after explosion rumbled through the innards of the great carrier, Admiral Nagumo acted as if in a trance. He refused to believe that his mighty ship, for six months the terror of the Pacific and arbiter of the fate of nations, had been fatally hit. Despite pleadings for him to leave the ship before it was too late, he adamantly refused to budge and maintained that there was still a good chance she could be saved.

By this time the continued explosions below and the resulting spreading of the fires had almost isolated the bridge from the rest of the ship and Nagumo and his staff looked like being cooked alive. In desperation Lieutenant Commander Nishbayashi, the admiral's flag lieutenant, reported that all escape passages below were on fire. The only way off the bridge was by means of a rope from the window down to the deck and then to the anchor deck.

Rear Admiral Kusaka reminded Nagumo that, although *Akagi* was doomed, the rest of his fleet was still intact and that they must be led. But even these appeals failed to move the stubborn, angry admiral, obsessed with the feeling of bitter defeat. In the end he had to be forcibly taken by the arms and led from the bridge of his beloved *Akagi.*

Scrambling down ropes and moving along smoke-shrouded and corpse-strewn passageways, they came at last to the port anchor deck and from here Nagumo and his senior staff officers were transferred, with some difficulty, to the light cruiser *Nagara*, flagship of the destroyer screen, in which he hoisted his flag. The ritual of transferring the Emperor's portrait was also undertaken, symbolising the acknowledgement of the end of the ship as a fighting vessel. This was done at 1715.

Like her sister, the *Akagi* lingered on for several hours in her final death agony. All the big fireproof doors had been shattered in the after hangar-decks by the force of the detonations, and likewise most of the pumps were put out of action. There was little the fire-fighting teams could do but they clung to their task tenaciously although ineffectively. The engine rooms of the giant vessel remained intact from the blasts and explosions. The engines had been rung down to stop, to assist in bringing the fires under control by preventing draught through the hangars, but, soon after this order had been complied with, the fires raging through the upper parts of the vessel had cut off all communications with the engine room. Listening to the thunder of the carnage above them and the muffled screams and cries of dying men, the engineers waited stoically for the order to abandon ship. The order never came, and even if it had there was no way for the men to get out.

Those above them had been forced from the flight deck, now a mass of fire and smoke, to the sanctuary of the anchor deck and it was from there that they began to abandon ship at 1915. The destroyers *Arashi* and *Nowaki* had been standing by to give what assistance they could, which was little or none in the circumstances, and began to pick up survivors from the water. *Akagi*'s commanding officer took care to see that this was done as effectively as possible, but he knew his ship could never survive. Rather than let her fall into enemy hands he wanted to destroy her and so, accordingly, he signalled to Nagumo for permission to send her to the bottom with torpedoes from the destroyers. This message was intercepted by Admiral Yamamoto who gave orders that this should be delayed. On receipt of this message Captain Aoki returned to his ship and there he lashed himself to the anchor. He would die with his vessel.

But once again the *Akagi* proved that the Japanese built tough ships. The twisted metal of the decks, the buckled lifts and the burnt-out bridge structure gave her the appearance of a nightmare vessel, but she stayed stubbornly afloat; below the waterline she was sound and intact, where beneath the raging fires her engineering complement and other trapped men still awaited orders to leave her.

Throughout the night she drifted and burned and news was received that the Americans had closed to within ninety miles of her. By now four Japanese destroyers stood by her as pallbearers at a melancholy funeral. Once, a hurrying squadron of warships passed close by, which led Captain Ariga to give chase, but they vanished into the night and it later was learnt that these were Japanese warships retreating. As dawn broke over the crippled carrier Yamamoto finally bowed to the inevitable and orders were given to put *Akagi* out of her misery. All four Japanese destroyers fired their torpedoes into the forlorn hulk just before first sunrise and the great carrier slipped below the waves. As she went under a final enormous underwater explosion was heard, the death rattle of the pride of the fleet and the final salute for over 270 of her crew who went down with her. Captain Aoki, however, had been persuaded to leave the ship and was taken aboard the *Nowaki* before the final act of the drama.

Thus passed *Akagi*.

The third victim of the Dauntless dive-bombers, the *Soryu*, proved equally resilient. Although a much smaller ship than *Akagi* and *Kaga*, she also took terrific punishment and stood up to it well.

Gallaher's bombers, with three of Best's planes, caught her with her deck parks full and as she was just about to turn into the wind to commence launching. The first explosions aboard the *Kaga* were the only warnings that the men aboard *Soryu* had about their own imminent fate and even before the stunned gunners had time to take in what this meant the first of three equally devastating bomb hits was made.

At 1026 the first bomb hit the flight-deck smack in the centre, just before the forward lift. Plunging through it, it exploded in the packed hangar below and the resulting blast tore out the huge lift and flung it disdainfully, a crumpled mass of steel, against the bridge island. The second and third bombs hit and penetrated the flight-deck further aft and produced the same carnage and bedlam as has been described aboard the other two carriers.

Once more the inside of the carrier was turned into a flaming inferno and men were struck down in scores by fire and flying splinters. The main engines came to a halt and the steering gear failed, while the bulk of fire appliances were destroyed before they could be brought into use. The ship was swept from stem to stern by flames and smoke.

Twenty minutes after this devastation another huge explosion took place below decks throwing men into the sea with its violence. The fires remounted with even greater fury. The captain realised that his command was doomed and gave the order to abandon ship, and the escorting destroyers *Hamakaze* and *Isokaze* closed to effect a rescue of the hundreds of men dotting the water around the blazing vessel.

Captain Yanagimoto elected to remain on board and was last seen on the bridge, ceremonial sword in hand, singing the national anthem in proud defiance of the fate which had taken his ship's life and which was shortly to claim his own.

However the *Soryu* remained afloat for a considerable time

considering the extent of her injuries and was still above water at 1913. But then, rent asunder by a series of further explosions, she rapidly went under, taking with her Captain Yanagimoto and more than 700 of her crew. Again, all her fine aircraft went into the depths with her.

Three great carriers crippled in as many minutes. It was a stunning moment. No other Japanese ship had been hit it was true but there was no denying that this was a deadly, indeed decisive, stroke. Four of the SBDs from Gallaher's squadron, seeing that *Soryu* had been decisively hit, had, in fact made their dives at an alternative target. This was not the *Hiryu*, who remained isolated and shielded to the north, but the battleship *Haruna*. Although they had to face a far greater volume of fire from this tough target, they nonetheless pressed their attacks home with equal valour. But all they did was near-miss *Haruna* which had no effect at all on her speed or fighting efficiency.

The cost to the SBDs was small and only four were shot down during the attack. There remained, for the elated pilots and crews, the difficult tasks of extricating themselves from the gunfire of the fully alerted fleet and making their way back across the long empty miles to locate their parent ships. In both these tasks the dive-bombers, once more, fared better than their earlier compatriots.

McClusky himself was set upon by a pair of Zero fighters in vengeful mood as he broke away from his own attack. The Japanese fighters that were airborne, though now few in number, were aided by the fact that they did not have to gain altitude now that the bombers were so low after their dives. Even so they were uniformly unsuccessful in exacting more than a token price from the Americans for their achievements.

Hugging the wave-tops at twenty-five feet McClusky was chased for 35 miles. Despite the fact that the Zeros filled his bomber with more than fifty shell and machine-gun holes the sturdy little Dauntless kept flying. McClusky was hit in the shoulder but his gunner, Chochalousek, managed to shoot down one of the Zeros and damage the other; a remarkable achievement. Another Zero was calmly shot down by gunner Floyd D. Atkins using his heavy machine-gun to good effect even though it had broken away from its cradle.

Leslie on the other hand brought his squadron away completely unscathed, again keeping low over the waves throughout the initial breakaway period. He also calculated the position of his carrier with great accuracy and got all his seventeen dive-bombers safely back on the route of the *Yorktown*. Unfortunately his arrival coincided with the return of Thach's fighters. These, having fought off larger numbers of Zeros and lost one of their number in so doing, were badly cut up and given the first priority to land on. Leslie's victorious SBDs therefore had to wait for this to be done. Thach brought Fletcher the first eyewitness description of the bombing and burning of three Japanese carriers which must have been highly elating and relieving news for the admiral. But again, before Leslie's bombers could come in, the first warnings of the incoming Japanese counter strike was reported and once more the Dauntless bombers were waved away.

McClusky and his group had not estimated the position of their carrier so precisely. In fact the estimated point of contact was worked out allowing the carriers a speed of approach to the battle scene of twenty-four knots, but, due to delays to turn into the wind to launch and recover aircraft, the carriers were delayed. Thus McClusky had to cast about him for the American carriers as he had earlier for the Japanese. He eventually picked up the *Yorktown*, then located the *Enterprise* and finally landed with two gallons of fuel remaining in his tanks. Most others were equally fortunate, but three SBDs had to ditch through lack of fuel.

Leslie's orphans continued to circle out of harm's way while the Japanese attack went in, and two of these bombers also had to ditch. The remainder put down on *Enterprise*.

There remained the mystery of the submarine that fired torpedoes at the dying *Kaga*.

This turned out to be the unshakable *Nautilus*. After surviving the attacks of *Arashi* earlier in the day, Lieutenant Commander Brockman had brought his command to the surface and set course at his best possible speed after the Japanese battle force in the hope of catching up with any crippled stragglers from the battle that was taking place to the north-east of him. It was a long, slow process for the elderly submarine but, at 1145, he was rewarded with the sight of smoke on the horizon.

He submerged and closed the remaining eight miles at periscope depth. After an hour he could confirm that it was indeed a burning Japanese aircraft-carrier. Although the stern of the ship was smashed up completely the fires seemed to be under control. It was a heaven-sent opportunity.

She only had two destroyers as escorts and they seemed to be fully preoccupied with survivors – his target was moving sluggishly through the water at two knots and some salvage attempts were in progress. Brockman noted that the carrier had a starboard-sided island and from this deduced that she was of the *Soryu* class. However here he was in error for his target was, with little doubt, the *Kaga*, a larger ship but which also carried a starboard island structure (*Akagi* carried hers to port).

Stalking his target carefully, he could not expect any more strokes of good fortune to follow this morning's events, he had got *Nautilus* into a good firing position by 1359.

From a distance of some 2700 yards *Nautilus* fired three deliberately aimed torpedoes at her vast target and Brockman was certain that all three were hits.

When he got back to periscope level at 1610, after undergoing a prolonged and severe depth-charge attack from both the destroyers, Brockman observed that she was burning along her entire length again and was convinced that he was responsible for this satisfactory state of affairs.

However this was not the case. As we shortly notice Japanese survivors in the water from the *Kaga* confirmed that this attack took place. At 1410, for example, Lieutenant Commander Yoshio Kunisada, a damage control officer, saw three torpedoes, marked quite clearly by their white wakes, heading straight for the *Kaga*, and was convinced that they must hit and destroy her. He closed his eyes and awaited the expected concussion and shock wave through the water which he knew would probably kill him and most of the other survivors in the water near by. Instead no concussion came.

One of the crew claimed to have witnessed this attack on the blazing carrier: 'The torpedo bounced off the side of the ship and several Japanese sailors clung to it.'

Commander Amagai, the flight officer of *Kaga*, was also in the water at this time and witnessed the same thing; he even sighted the periscope of the *Nautilus* as she made her attack. Despite the slowness of the target, and the deliberateness of his attack, Brockman had, in fact, been unrewarded. Two of the torpedoes ran wide while the third, as we have seen, hit the carrier at too acute an angle, bounced off and remained floating, to be utilised as a life raft by several of the carrier's crew. The fires rekindled themselves internally and were not caused by external hits, all eye-witnesses agree on this point. The combat report of the Nagumo force itself reports that a submarine torpedo attack was made on *Kaga* at this time (1110 Tokyo time, 1410 Midway time) and that no hits were made or damage resulted.

Brockman's identification of the target as *Soryu* led most post-war writers, including Morison, to dismiss the reports of the *Kaga*'s crew and the official Japanese version, but since that time most serious researchers into the battle have accepted the point of view that it was in fact *Kaga* that *Nautilus* attacked unsuccessfully at this time. This is of course no reflection on Brockman and his crew, who behaved with valour and skill that day, it might be a reflection on the condition of the American torpedoes of this time however!

At 1020 the Nagumo force was steaming proud and intact – at 1030 three of its four carriers were blazing wrecks and his command lay in ruins! What could Nagumo do now to rectify this terrible position?

It will be remembered that the admiral had finally been taken aboard the light cruiser *Nagara* after a lot of argument. But even before this he had refused to contemplate the possibility of defeat. He transferred operational control for tactical orders to Rear Admiral Abe, commanding the battleship and cruiser force, with orders to strike back at the Americans.

In truth Abe had little left to do so with. Only the *Hiryu* remained with her intact striking force, and she was one of his smaller carriers. Nonetheless he determined to do what he could to retrieve the position. Although he only had one carrier and the Americans had at least two and possibly more, he decided to attack at once.

One point in the Japanese favour was that the Americans had suffered fearful casualties in the air and even though they might have the carriers, they could not still have very many aircraft. If the Japanese could hit the American ships in the same manner as they had just been hit, while the returning American planes were landing on and being refuelled and re-armed, they might yet turn the tables.

Air operations passed automatically to Rear Admiral Yamaguchi aboard *Hiryu*, and he reported to Abe aboard the heavy cruiser *Tone* that he was ready to launch his first wave. Abe agreed and signalled to the very worried commander-in-chief, still many miles astern aboard the *Yamato*:

'Sighted enemy composed of one carrier, five cruisers and six destroyers at position bearing 10°, 240 miles from Midway. We are heading for it.'

From the flight-deck of the *Hiryu* at 1100 rose the first attack wave – eighteen Val dive-bombers with six Zero fighters as escort. This wave was led by Lieutenant Michio Kobayashi and were soon setting off eastward. Despite their very modest fighter escort of all that could be spared, they were confident, for Kobayashi was one of their ablest squadron leaders. Their target was the *Yorktown*.

Meanwhile the Japanese were closing ranks in order to present a powerful front to the Americans. From Admiral Kondo came a signal to Nagumo telling him that he was bringing his strong force of battleships and cruisers up to his aid. From Admiral Yamamoto came word that he was bringing down the light carriers *Ryujo* and *Junyo* from the north to join *Hiryu*. The great battleships of Vice Admiral Takasu's Aleutians screening force was being ordered to rejoin *Yamato* and her consorts to form a battle line still unequalled in the Pacific. If only this massive concentration had taken place before the events of 4 June instead of after! It would take days for the concentration to take place, and the Japanese had bare hours to retrieve the situation as it stood now.

Meanwhile the scouting aircraft from the cruiser *Chikuma* had *Yorktown* and her group in constant surveillance and transmitted a steady stream of homing reports for *Hiryu*'s dive-bombers as they made their long approach. Yamaguchi's flyers however were to be denied any element of surprise for Fletcher picked up the incoming Vals at forty miles' range on *Yorktown*'s radar screen.

It was close on noon when the approaching Japanese formation was sighted to the south-west at high level. The combat air patrol of *VF-3*, led by those of Thach's squadron that had remained behind, was at once homed on to the Vals and they had the height and time to intercept while still some twenty miles away from the ships.

Yorktown herself cracked on to thirty knots, the screen opened up, all guns straining for maximum elevation and range. All the vulnerable fuel lines were emptied and an auxiliary fuel tank with 800 gallons of aviation spirit was dumped overboard. Up on the bridge Admiral Fletcher awaited the attack. He had had his crack and had scored magnificently, now the ball was in the Japanese court and all he could do was sit and take it. *Yorktown*'s group was as ready as it could be and the Japanese attack was not a large one.

Kobayashi's formation had in fact picked up several homecoming torpedo-bombers from the American strike and followed these returning aircraft right down the line to the American carrier. Unfortunately the temptation of this proved too strong for two of his escorting fighters who broke away to make attacks on them. This left the eighteen very vulnerable Vals with only four Zeros to protect them and when the twelve Wildcats pounced they overwhelmed the Japanese defences.

From the American carriers the slaughter of the Japanese dive-bombers was witnessed with grim satisfaction. Ten of the dive-bombers fell blazing into the sea leaving long smoke trails behind them, or else were so badly shot up that they had to jettison their bombs and retire as best they could. Nothing the four Zeros could do could halt the massacre. It seemed as if the attack must surely fail but, against all the odds, eight of the Japanese dive-bombers broke through the defending cordon and came in high over the task force.

Every gun aboard the *Yorktown* and her escorting cruisers and destroyers was now firing flat-out filling the sky above the force with a wall of bursting shells. It seemed as if nothing could survive in that vast barrage, but, undeterred, the Vals kept boring in.

The *Astoria* and *Portland*, together with the main batteries of the destroyers, nailed two of these as they came plummeting down towards the carrier. The remaining six completed their dives and the *Yorktown* vanished in a flurry of exploding bombs, huge splashes from the near-misses and the death trail of another Val. This aircraft was shot through and through but continued to come straight in at the carrier's flight-deck. Just before it fell into blazing fragments its 500lb bomb fell free and smashed into the starboard side of the flight-deck close by number two lift, gouging out a huge hole and scything down gunners at the gun positions. A portion of blazing wing from the Val hit the deck and fragmented. Large fires were started below decks but the prompt and efficient use of the fire curtains, which remained fortunately intact, prevented the spreading of the flames and they were brought quickly under control.

The next direct hit penetrated the flight-deck from the port side and exploded in the funnel of the ship. Burning soot and paint cascaded over the carrier's island and deep inside the *Yorktown* two of her boilers were badly damaged in the uptakes and five of the six were put out. Speed fell away to six knots and then, some twenty minutes after this hit, the American carrier slid to a standstill, a sitting duck.

Yet a third direct hit was scored by the Vals, this latter plunging in through the starboard side of the ship and penetrating to the fourth deck where it detonated, setting ablaze the rag stowage compartment which was right next to the forward magazines. These were promptly flooded, thus preventing a similar catastrophe to that which had torn the Japanese ships asunder earlier.

Only five of the Japanese dive-bombers survived this gallant attack to return to the *Hiryu*. Their sacrifice was magnificent but still the *Yorktown* was not out of the fight by any means. True, her radar had been knocked out and her communications system shot to hell, but she was still seaworthy, although unable to launch or recover her aircraft.

The damage that she had sustained meant that Admiral Fletcher, like Admiral Nagumo before him, was forced to make a hurried and undignified shift of flag. He moved over to the cruiser *Astoria* and took command of his own group from there. With *Yorktown* out of the fight, Fletcher gave Rear Admiral Spruance a free hand with the flying operations.

The *Portland* was ordered to take the crippled *Yorktown* in tow and head for Pearl Harbor, and the cruisers *Pensacola* and *Vincennes* with destroyers *Benham* and *Balch* were sent over by Spruance to reinforce the *Yorktown* screen against further attacks.

Aboard the carrier her damage control parties worked like furies to repair their gallant vessel. They worked to such good effect at this task, to which they were becoming veterans by now, that at 1340 she was able to signal that she was back under her own control. Four boilers were again operative and soon she was able to work up to about eighteen knots speed; a splendid achievement. It was at this time however that the second wave of the *Hiryu*'s attack put in their appearance.

Once again it was a weak attack but all that the Japanese had left. Ten Kate torpedo-bombers and six Zero fighters was the sum total of this effort.

This small force was launched by 1331 and headed off in the wake of the dive-bombers. They were led by Lieutenant Joichi Tomonaga of *Hiryu* and included one Kate from *Akagi* and two Zero fighters from *Kaga* that had found refuge aboard *Hiryu* earlier. Tomonaga, as we have seen, had led the Midway strike and his plane had been damaged in that raid. The left fuel tank had been punctured and no time had been left to effect its repair. That left the Kate with enough fuel only for a one-way trip. Tomonaga accepted this without demur, he was going to his death. Those that followed this very brave man can have had few illusions either of just what they were up against, for by now the Nagumo force had details of just what size a fleet the Americans were operating.

Before the devastating American attack, the *Soryu* had flown off one of her special high-speed reconnaissance aircraft to make contact and bring more detailed news of the enemy than

130

had been received from any of the floatplanes. This aircraft had arrived back aboard the *Hiryu* and carried startling news. Its radio had failed but the pilot reported that the Americans were operating *three* carriers for certain, which he correctly identified as *Enterprise*, *Hornet* and *Yorktown*!

The five surviving Vals arrived back aboard and reported that they had left one American carrier ablaze although they were not certain how badly damaged she was. What was very obvious however was that *Hiryu* was facing odds of at least three to one.

Just before 1430 Tomonaga's force found the *Yorktown*, apparently as good as new with fighters on deck and moving through the water. After the reports of the Vals that the carrier had been left burning heavily from several bomb hits it was not surprising that the Japanese believed this to be another carrier and not the same one that was taken under attack by the second wave.

Eight Wildcats got off *Yorktown*'s decks and joined the four fighters already in the sky to make the interception. When first picked up, again by radar, this time from the escorting cruisers, the Japanese formation was about thirty-three miles out from the ships and closing fast. They were twenty miles away when the Wildcats closed with them but this time the defending Zeros put up a better show in defence and the bulk of the torpedo-bombers were able, at 1432, to split into groups to press home their attacks from different angles as if on exercises. At very low level they bore in over the destroyer screen towards the sluggishly moving carrier, and, despite powerful flak from the reinforced defences, some broke through.

Behind them three of the Zeros fell flaming into the sea, but they had done their job. The ten torpedo-bombers now had only the ships' guns between them and their objective. The heavy cruisers *Astoria*, *Pensacola*, *Portland* and *Vincennes* had been stationed by Rear Admiral Smith in box formation around the *Yorktown* to give her maximum protection, and when she turned hard right they complied, keeping the box intact.

As the Japanese torpedo-bombers were coming in very low a heavy 'splash barrage' was laid down in their paths with the four big cruisers firing their 8in guns, as well as their 5in anti-aircraft batteries and lighter weapons, to throw up a wall of water in the path of the Kates. Nothing was expected to penetrate such a screen, and indeed caught between this and the flak from the destroyer screen, five of the Kates were destroyed, including the gallant Tomonaga.

His aircraft was seen to release its torpedo before it was torn apart by the flak but four Kates survived it all and pressed in to within 500 yards of the *Yorktown* before launching their torpedoes. One pilot was even seen shaking his fist in defiance as he pulled out through the screen!

One of the *Yorktown* Wildcats was barely clear of the flight-deck with his wheels still down when this attack came in. He swung right, fired a burst at a Kate, was hit with machine-gun fire from a Zero and belly-flopped back in the water, all in less than a minute.

Meanwhile *Yorktown* was manoeuvring as best she could to avoid the four torpedoes speeding towards her. She was unable to escape however. At 1442, having evaded two of them, the carrier shuddered as the others hit home on her port side.

The rudder jammed hard left and all power died away. Most of her fuel tanks were breached and she immediately took on a seventeen-degree list. Without the necessary power counter-flooding was impossible and within half an hour of taking these two fish in her stomach the *Yorktown* was heeling over at the alarming angle of twenty-six degrees. It seemed extremely probable that she was about to capsize. At 1456 therefore Captain Buckmaster gave the order to abandon ship and into the smooth water splashed the bulk of *Yorktown*'s crew. Four destroyers closed in and began picking them up while the other escorts prowled round frustratedly to give her what further protection they could.

At 1630 the surviving Japanese aircraft returned to the *Hiryu*. Only five Kates and three Zeros returned. Apart from a solitary message broadcast at 1445 claiming two torpedo hits on a *Yorktown* class carrier no news had reached Yamaguchi of the fate of his airmen. The survivors were questioned closely about their attack. They claimed that they had in fact hit a carrier, damaged a heavy cruiser, and shot down eight American fighters.

Yamaguchi therefore held high hopes that two American carriers had been damaged, a splendid performance by his own air group, if true, and that he might therefore only have to face one enemy carrier. Once *Junyo* and *Ryujo* joined him he would be able to resume the offensive with the support of the battleships. Victory might yet be achieved despite the crushing setback of the morning. He had only to keep *Hiryu* afloat until the next day to retrieve the situation. Alas, the Japanese strikes, although in themselves splendid, had not achieved his hopes. Retribution was already on its way.

Nor could *Hiryu* do much else other than remain out of the Americans' way if she could, for she had nothing left to fight with. Her total aircraft complement consisted of five Vals, four Kates and six Zeros and their crews were exhausted. All this Yamaguchi knew, but he still determined to make another strike with these survivors against what he hoped was the last American carrier. A daylight attack with such meagre strength was out of the question but he had hopes that a dusk attack might get through. Could he but damage the last American carrier the Japanese battleships would have no trouble in deciding the course of the battle when it was resumed in the morning. Accordingly the *Hiryu* prepared for one last desperate sortie. It was never to take place.

Even before the Japanese had counter-attacked against the *Yorktown*, Admiral Fletcher was searching for the *Hiryu*. Scout planes had been sent out to hunt her down, ten SBDs under Lieutenant Wallace C. Short had been combing the area north of the morning's battle zone and, at 1445, one of them, piloted by Samuel Adams, was rewarded with the sight of the *Hiryu*, the two battleships, three cruisers and four destroyers some 110 miles north-west of *Yorktown*. The estimate of the composition of Yamaguchi's force was spot-on and was received aboard the *Enterprise* with joy.

At 1530 therefore Spruance launched a strike force of twenty-four SBDs from *Enterprise* while the *Hornet* put into the sky at the same time a further sixteen dive-bombers. No fighters could be spared to escort them, like the Japanese the Americans were coming to the end of their resources; what Wildcats

133

remained were held back for fighter cover for the carriers themselves.

Hornet's attack group went off at 1603 and attacked independently, but it was the redoubtable McClusky, with his two dozen veterans of the morning attacks, who eventually found *Hiryu* at 1700 that afternoon.

Aboard the *Hiryu* preparations were in hand at 1703 for the launching of a scout plane to pinpoint the American carrier in readiness for the dusk attack. A fighter patrol was aloft but failed to sight the Americans approach.

The SBDs attacked from out of the setting sun and caught them completely off guard for the second time that day. The *Hiryu* and her escorts began to open fire but the Dauntless bombers were already tipping over and commencing their dives. The carrier speeded up to thirty knots and put her wheel hard over to the starboard to commence a full circle. But before she was very far into it the first bombs began to hit her.

The first three bombs were avoided by this turn it is true but there were far too many dive-bombers for her to avoid her fate. At 1703 the first of four devastating hits ploughed into the forward flight-deck and three others followed in rapid succession. The forward elevator platform was blasted from its seating to crash against the bridge, wrecking it. All the deck in front of this lift was convulsed and warped upward shutting out the view ahead. Nothing remained of the flight-deck forward save for a vast smoking and flaming inferno as the other three bombs smashed straight into her now unprotected vitals, causing the usual horrific fires. The dead and dying lay in piles and the suffocating smoke from the oil fires began to seep aft throughout the whole lower deck levels of the carrier. Aircraft began to blow up and spread destruction further.

Around her the anti-aircraft fire strengthened and three Dauntless bombers were hit and crashed flaming into the sea but it was by that time too late for *Hiryu*. Seeing she was doomed some SBDs again turned their attentions to the looming bulks of the battleships and heavy cruisers whose sides belched fire from scores of guns. *Haruna* was again near-missed for the umpteenth time already in this war and was not hurt at all.

Hornet's bombers attacked at 1732 and again they chose the heavy ships of the screen as their targets with no more luck than the others. The *Chikuma* was singled out for an attack by nine Dauntless dive-bombers at this time and came through unscathed and unshaken. Likewise the *Tone* was taken under attack by three SBDs at 1720, and nine more at 1728, and came through it all unmarked.

Meanwhile aboard the stricken *Hiryu* the flames were taking control. Admiral Yamaguchi signalled to Nagumo and told him that he was abandoning ship. The muster was sounded and about half the crew of 1500 men were left alive to respond to it. The time was 0315 on the morning of 5 June, some eight hours after her bombing. Yet again, the carrier, although devastated, had proved a hard nut to actually sink.

The Fortresses of the USAAF had earlier claimed to have done so, at 1810 in fact. Twelve B-17s under the command of Major G. A. Blakey and Lieutenant Colonel Sweeney took part and all dropped at *Hiryu*, one Fort even coming down to make a strafing run. They claimed the usual hits but in fact made none at all.

A sortie by the valiant Midway-based Vindicators of the USMC under their new leader, Major Benjamin W. Norris, together with five SBDs, ten dive-bombers in all, went out from the atoll's airstrip at 1900 to make a night attack on the blazing carrier but failed to find her. Major Norris did not come back from this sortie.

They were not needed. Although he had ordered abandon ship Admiral Yamaguchi informed his surviving officers that he himself had no intention whatsoever of leaving. The transfer of the Emperor's portrait took place. The ship's captain, Captain Kaku, also decided to share the fate of his command and of his admiral. The rescue destroyers pulled away from the burnt-out hull, listing some fifteen degrees, to administer the *coup de grâce*. Torpedoes sped from the tubes of the *Kazagumo* and *Yugumo* at 0510 that morning and exploded against the carrier's sides. The resulting explosions confirmed, or seemed to confirm, that her fate was sealed and the senior destroyer officer, Captain Abe, accordingly withdrew his ships, reporting to Yamamoto that *Hiryu* had been scuttled in accordance with orders. The destroyers vanished over the horizon, but *Hiryu* remained stubbornly afloat!

And what of the commander-in-chief of the Japanese forces while these momentous events were taking place? How did the picture now seem to him?

By placing himself so far from the actual point of contact Yamamoto made a rod for his own back. He had to rely totally on diverse fragments of intercepted radio reports, sightings and what information the men on the spot chose to convey to him. His forces were scattered all over the central and northern Pacific and the Americans appeared to be winning hands-down despite his paper superiority over them. His most cherished and hard-fought-for plan was falling to pieces about his ears. It was hardly the news to end his stomach troubles!

As we have seen he had at once taken steps to rectify the most obvious of his mistakes and was now hoping to reverse the day's results by a policy of concentration. But much of what he had planned to do depended on resolute leadership from his subordinates. Most of his admirals were adamant that all was not yet lost and that their forces could sweep east and wipe out the Americans despite the loss of the four big carriers. There were still four Japanese carriers in the field, albeit small ones, and if they could combine, that should be sufficient against one lone American carrier whose air strength must, they reasoned, be now almost completely exhausted.

However Nagumo was himself to pour cold water on these hopes. On transferring to the light cruiser *Nagara* he was informed, at 1130, by the *Chikuma* scout plane, that the location of the American fleet was only some ninety miles from his own force. Only seven cruisers and five destroyers were thought to be with the American carrier or carriers. Nagumo's two fast battleships and two heavy cruisers, with their screening destroyers, should therefore be able to quickly close with them and bring them to decisive battle. This is the view that the senior staff officer, Captain Oishi, put forward at that time, and, after some consideration, Admiral Nagumo agreed. He signalled to his ships to assemble in readiness, 'We will go to the attack now.'

To emphasise the importance of speed the signal was repeated twice, at 1156 and 1159. The *Nagara* came round to a north-easterly course to rendezvous with the heavy ships. Admiral Kondo, who was steaming to join him, was likewise informed of the situation as it then was, with three carriers inoperational.

This burst of defiant courage in Admiral Nagumo however was of short duration. Further sighting reports kept coming in and these, coupled with his own losses, gradually had the effect of eating away at his self-confidence. The *Tone*'s aircraft signalled at 1300 that the Americans were withdrawing, in order, it was assumed, to keep the Japanese surface ships at safe distance and wear them down with air strikes. The immediate daylight action was therefore reconsidered and rejected as impracticable. Instead Nagumo substituted a night action when any air superiority the American fleet might still have, would be completely nullified. Accordingly Nagumo decided that, instead of dashing fearlessly to the east, he would retire to the west for a time and regroup.

Then came news of the destruction of the *Hiryu* and with her the last vestige of air support for his fleet. It should not have altered the decision on the validity of the night action, but it did so. It was the final straw that broke Nagumo's confidence in himself and in his command. His subsequent signals reflected that. When, at 1733, another message from shadowing aircraft confirmed that Fletcher was not prepared to walk into any such trap against superior surface forces but was wisely keeping out of reach of Nagumo's heavy guns even the hopes of a night action faded.

What finally put the tin hat on any such aggressive action by the Nagumo force was a message taken in at 1830 from *Chikuma*. Her floatplane reported that at 1713 it had sighted the American fleet and that it now consisted of *four* carriers, six cruisers and fifteen destroyers and that they were on a westerly course. Four carriers! It seemed impossible. But after the day's shattering events Nagumo was now prepared to believe only the worst. Perhaps it *was* true, and if there were four carriers still intact heading west, it could only mean that further devastating air strikes were on their way towards him. It was enough, despite protests from Oishi that they should go ahead

137

with the night action, Nagumo threw in the towel. His ships came about and set course for home.

Yamamoto was equally undeterred earlier on in the afternoon. He also refused to acknowledge that the fight was lost, far from it. From the bridge of the *Yamato* he sent a stirring – and somewhat over-optimistic – signal to all fleet commanders:

1 The enemy fleet, *which has practically been destroyed*, is retiring to the east.
2 Combined fleet units in the vicinity are preparing to pursue the remnants and at the same time to occupy Midway.
3 The main body is scheduled to reach lat 32° 10′ N long 175° 43′ E, on course 90°, speed 20 knots, by midnight.
4 The mobile force, occupation forces (less crusier division 7) and advance force will immediately contact and attack the enemy.

Stirring stuff indeed. Cruiser division 7, Admiral Kurita's four big cruisers, had been ordered to go ahead at full speed and commence a pulverising bombardment of Midway atoll. Then, at 2130 the signal bridge of the *Yamato* took in the following signal from Nagumo:

'Total enemy strength is *five* carriers, six heavy cruisers and fifteen destroyers. They are steaming westwards. We are retiring to the north-west escorting *Hiryu*. Speed 18 knots.'

So now Nagumo had added the burning *Yorktown* to the already inaccurate account and had not mentioned the fact that she was damaged. It gave the impression that five fully combat-ready carriers were steaming hard on his tail. And yet, as we have seen, he knew the American ships to be withdrawing not attacking.

Rear Admiral Ugaki voiced the feelings of the entire staff aboard *Yamato*, when he saw that message; it was obvious that Nagumo's nerve had gone and that he was piling horror upon horror to justify his action in calling off the night engagement. 'The Nagumo force has no stomach for a night engagement,' commented Ugaki, and he was right. All that now concerned Nagumo was to extricate himself with the minimum delay from the scene of his defeat. His signal mentioned the fact that they were escorting the damaged *Hiryu* as they fled, but in fact the ships of the Nagumo force cracked on at such a rate that that solitary carrier was soon left very far astern with only two destroyers as company.

At 2250 another edgy and defeatist signal came over the ocean from *Nagara* to *Yamato*. Like its predecessor it did nothing to improve the commander-in-chief's frame of mind or restore his confidence in his striking force leader. Nagumo stated flatly:

'There still exist four enemy carriers . . . six cruisers and sixteen destroyers. These are steaming westward. None of our carriers are operational.'

Yamamoto had had enough of this type of talk. Admiral Kondo, who was hurrying northward to join Nagumo with his battleships, was told to take over from Nagumo, who was told to take command of the abandoned and sinking carriers. From being the kingpin of the whole operation this summary demotion to glorified salvage organiser was the final bitter humiliation for Admiral Nagumo. 4 June was indeed the blackest day in his life. He never regained the high prestige that he had enjoyed up to that day.

Admiral Kondo was made of much sterner stuff, he still had confidence in his gunners and their night-fighting training. That that confidence was not misplaced was to be proved over and over again during the battles around Guadalcanal and the Solomon Islands later that year, but, at Midway, his ships were never to be given the opportunity to prove themselves. At 2340 Kondo was signalling the ships under him to prepare themselves for immediate night action. Three hours later came the news that Yamamoto had suffered the same misgivings as the unfortunate Nagumo. He too was getting very cold feet!

CHAPTER SIX

THE FOG OF WAR

If Admiral Yamamoto was faced with an agonising decision during the night of 4–5 June, then it was a decision he had to take alone. At home in Tokyo the naval general staff, having given him his head over the Midway operation about which they had grave reservations, were following the news of the disasters of the day but nobody acted to get Yamamoto off the hook. In one way it was a very commendable attitude to take; history has taught over and over again that vital decisions in battle must be taken by the man on the spot (a decision taken in London the next month about the action to be taken by a naval force in a similar dilemma had ghastly consequences as the well-known story of PQ 17 has shown).

On the other hand it could be said that Yamamoto, having played his hunches to the hilt, was to be left to face the consequences of his actions alone. It was still his ball game even though it had all turned very sour on him.

Further discussions took place on *Yamato*'s bridge that night but, as it became increasingly clear that, despite all their endeavours, there was little chance of bringing the cagey Americans to battle that night, enthusiasm for the full-speed dash eastward into the unknown began to wane.

Various alternative proposals were put forward to salvage something from the wreck.

The most popular plan was for a composite air striking force, to be made up from the small air complements of the *Hosho* of Yamamoto's force and the *Zuiho* of Kondo's fleet, with additional aircraft from the battleships' and cruisers' scout planes.

Another viewpoint was that the proposed bombardment at

dawn by Kurita's four cruisers should be further expanded by the inclusion of the Japanese battleships themselves. Such an overwhelming weight of gunfire would be certain of neutralising Midway's airstrip while the battleships would stand off the carriers' air attacks on their own. Rear Admiral Ugaki rejected this out of hand. He was of the opinion that to pit battleships against shore batteries was folly and that to pit battleships against bombers was suicidal. In both cases he enormously over-estimated the American defences and the damage that they were capable of inflicting on such a force, but his cold water scotched that idea also.

Admiral Yamamoto began to hedge. At 0015 he issued orders from his flagship that Kondo's combined force, instead of heading eastward in search of the enemy, should instead ' . . . join the main body'.

At 0250 he followed this up with the decision to send the still-floating *Akagi* to the bottom. He appeared resigned to defeat. Five minutes later, at 0255 on 5 June, he issued the final set of instructions which made it clear that the Midway attack was over. It read:

1 The Midway operation is cancelled.
2. The main body will assemble the Midway invasion force and the first carrier striking force (less *Hiryu* and her escorts), and the combined forces will carry out refuelling during the morning. (Position given.)
3 The screening force, *Hiryu* and her escorts, and *Nisshin* will proceed to join (the others at refuelling position).
4 The transport group will proceed westward out of range of Midway-based planes.

It only remained for the Japanese to extricate themselves without further losses. But even this was to be denied them.

Meanwhile the American admirals had been faced with a simliar problem. They knew the extent of the power that lay out there beyond Midway atoll and, although they were cheered by the reports of the bombing and burning of no less than four big enemy carriers, to risk pushing their slender forces out into those wastes in search of the remains of the Japanese fleet might result in a catch too big for them to handle!

Since the damage to the *Yorktown* and his enforced shift of flag to *Astoria*, Admiral Fletcher had wisely allowed Rear Admiral Spruance to handle the air strikes from his still-operational carriers, contenting himself for the moment to merely '... conform to your movements.'

Reports received from the late afternoon attacking B-17s contained details of interception attempts by Zero fighters. These had probably flown off *Hiryu* before she was hit, but it could well be that another, as yet unlocated and undamaged, Japanese carrier was operational out there. Then there were the heavy ships moving up which might well have carriers with them (and of course in fact did). With his own air striking forces severely reduced Spruance was determined not to risk his remaining carriers in a night encounter with Yamamoto's heavy metal.

Admiral Spruance therefore did not boldly penetrate westward after his enemy but instead withdrew to the east until midnight. As he later wrote in his summing up:

'I wished to have a position from which either to follow up retreating enemy forces or to break up a landing attack on Midway.' This position he now gained for himself. Although he was to be criticised later for this action by those without knowledge of the Japanese intentions it can be seen that by refusing to play the enemy game Spruance acted with the utmost wisdom. It opened a wide gap between the two fleets once Yamamoto decided also to pull out, but it ensured that the resumption of the battle in the morning was once more to be decided by American aircraft against Japanese ships and not, as would have been fatal, against battleships with only heavy cruisers.

However for one Japanese force the decision to pull out came rather too late to save them from ordeal by fire, indeed the very order to withdraw involved them in a bloody battle.

It will be recalled that earlier on the night of 4 June, Yamamoto was still determined to press on with the actual invasion of Midway and, in preparation for this, he had instructed the cruiser squadron of Vice Admiral Kurita to close the islands by 0200 and commence a detailed bombardment of what remained of the defences there.

This mission Kurita was well able to comply with. He had under his command four of the most powerful heavy cruisers in the world which between them could lay down a pulverising barrage from their forty 8in guns. Against such a concentration of fire the American defenders could have made no reply by night, being outranged, and their aircraft would have been ineffective.

To open the ball, and keep the Americans guessing and worn out until the heavy ships arrived, the submarine *I-168* was also ordered to close Midway atoll and make a noise with her little gun. This Commander Tanabe commenced to do at 0130 after making a three-hour reconnaissance around the atoll. For the defenders the arrival of the first shell from *I-168* was an unpleasant surprise. They had made good much of the damage caused by the air strike suffered at dawn the previous day and enough aircraft were combat-ready to ensure that they would give a fair account of themselves should the Japanese invasion convoy arrive off Midway at dawn. However there was precious little they could do against a prolonged bombardment at night.

Fortunately for them *I-168* was no Kurita, her little gun made small effect and even those shells she did get off were way off target, not one hit the airstrip, most landed in the lagoon. The marine gunners were fully alert and within a short while were responding to the Japanese submarine's audacious assault with considerable fire-power. The water around the atoll became churned up with medium-calibre shells and Tanabe felt that, even though these were aimed with as little accuracy as his own, he was no opponent for such massed gun power. Accordingly he very prudently withdrew and submerged. *I-168* had fired eight shells, the marines forty-two. Nothing had been hit or damaged. The bombardment of Midway was over!

The recall signal sent out by Yamamoto had not reached *I-168* which was still awaiting the arrival of Kurita. He would soon silence the American defences, or so Tanabe thought, but in fact, while he was carrying out his lonely duel with the marines, Kurita's four heavy cruisers, *Kumano*, *Mikuma*, *Mogami* and *Suzuya*, with their escorting destroyers, *Arashio* and *Asashio*, were already in deep trouble some ninety miles only from Midway.

Although *I-168* remained in the vicinity of Midway until dawn of 5 June no support ever reached her. Disappointed, Tanabe hung on hopefully until the dawn air patrols from the atoll sighted him and subjected him to heavy depth-charge attacks.

The Japanese submarine survived these also but finally Tanabe came to the conclusion that the scheduled invasion was not going to take place. Unprepared to take on Midway on his own any longer, he submerged and loped off northwards in search of a damaged American carrier reported to be 150 miles to the north. His persistence and refusal to give up in the face of continued disappointments were to have their just reward later.

Admiral Kurita meanwhile had been racing through the night at full speed eager to get to Midway before dawn and start his bombardment. News of the grievous losses suffered by the Nagumo force acted as an added spur to the threat of air attack at sunrise. He was determined that his ships would restore the honour of the Imperial Navy. So hard did he push his heavy cruisers on that they even outpaced the two destroyer escorts who were left astern. Kurita was taking a chance that his high speed would give him the necessary immunity from American submarine attack, and in this he was right, but the thought of four big ships alone in waters that must be infested with enemy submarines was on everyone's mind as they roared through the night. Not unexpectedly everyone was very submarine-conscious, and they were on the alert the whole time and ready to react swiftly.

The orders to cancel their desperate mission reached the speeding squadron just before midnight. Plans were being discussed aboard Kurita's flagship which involved, if the bombardment failed, the sending ashore of a 'death-or-glory' landing party to destroy what installations they could. The consequent abandonment of their task when so near caused deep disappointment but Kurita had no choice but to obey.

Now he was really out on his own. By closing the island he at least stood some chance that his barrage would destroy the bulk of the aircraft on the open strip before they could get into the sky to attack him. By turning back so close to the target the American airmen were granted complete immunity of their base and aircraft, and Kurita himself would be faced with everything they cared to throw at him, and they had most of the daylight hours of the 5th in which to do it unless he could speedily get out of range or under the protection of a Japanese carrier. He had the worst of both worlds to face.

The four big cruisers came round on their retirement course and joined their two destroyers, but they were not unobserved.

Three American submarines remained to the west of Midway and one of these, the *Tambor* (Lieutenant Commander J. W. Murphy) picked them up as they made their turn. *Tambor* tried to close for an attack but her chances looked slim. Murphy nevertheless persisted and, at 0342, was sighted by the Japanese ships some four degrees off their starboard bow. Murphy had just sent off his first contact report after making sure the force was in fact hostile, but his report merely indicated 'many hostile ships'. He could not get in a good attacking position, but he didn't have to, his appearance so close to the keyed-up Japanese squadron had the same effect as a well-directed salvo of torpedoes.

Aboard the flagship *Kumano*, leading the line, reaction was swift and an emergency 45 degree turn to port was ordered. The signal was flashed to the next astern, *Suzuya*, who relayed it to *Mikuma* behind her by two low-powered signal lamps. The three leading ships therefore complied at once but the last of the line, *Mogami*, missed the signal and did not conform. The results of this were instant and tragic. Holding her original course the *Mogami* ploughed on straight into the port quarter of the *Mikuma*.

Although the cruisers had reduced speed to twenty-eight knots from thirty-three during their redeployment, it was still sufficiently high to ensure that the collision was a bad one.

Mogami's bows were crumpled back in a rending crash of

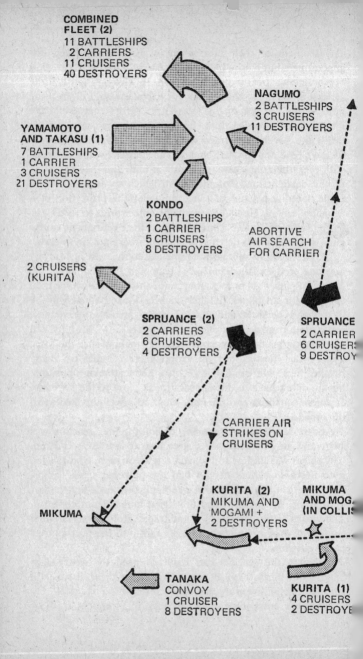

COMBINED FLEET (2)
11 BATTLESHIPS
2 CARRIERS
11 CRUISERS
40 DESTROYERS

NAGUMO
2 BATTLESHIPS
3 CRUISERS
11 DESTROYERS

YAMAMOTO AND TAKASU (1)
7 BATTLESHIPS
1 CARRIER
3 CRUISERS
21 DESTROYERS

KONDO
2 BATTLESHIPS
1 CARRIER
5 CRUISERS
8 DESTROYERS

ABORTIVE AIR SEARCH FOR CARRIER

2 CRUISERS (KURITA)

SPRUANCE (2)
2 CARRIERS
6 CRUISERS
4 DESTROYERS

SPRUANCE
2 CARRIER
6 CRUISER
9 DESTROY

CARRIER AIR STRIKES ON CRUISERS

MIKUMA

KURITA (2)
MIKUMA AND MOGAMI +
2 DESTROYERS

**MIKUMA AND MOG.
(IN COLLIS**

TANAKA
CONVOY
1 CRUISER
8 DESTROYERS

KURITA (1)
4 CRUISERS
2 DESTROYE

MIDWAY 3

FINAL MOVES OF THE
BATTLE — YORKTOWN,
HAMMANN AND MIKUMA
SUNK — BOTH SIDES
WITHDRAW

NOT TO SCALE

I.168  **YORKTOWN**

HAMMANN

 **FLETCHER**
2 CRUISERS
4 DESTROYERS

RESCUE
SHIPS, TUGS
AND DESTROYERS

MIDWAY

SHORE-BASED
AIR ATTACKS
ON CRUISERS

pulverised steel, the hull forward buckling back as far as 'A' gun turret. The smashed section caught fire and her speed fell away. The *Mikuma* had her hull ripped open and her port fuel tanks ruptured. Although she was able to maintain her speed she left a long trail of oil in her wake, a perfect pointer for questing American airmen at dawn. Eventually the *Mogami*, by running her engines for twenty-five knots, managed to achieve a speed of sixteen.

Kurita turned his force back in support. It was clear that the two cripples stood no chance of being clear of these very dangerous waters by daylight, but there was a chance they could struggle on to safety. Kurita decided not to risk his whole squadron; leaving the destroyers in attendance he hurried on to the west at his full speed to safety.

At twelve knots *Mogami* and *Mikuma* followed on. Behind them the sky lightened.

Meanwhile the cause of this accident, the *Tambor*, despite the crippled position of the two heavy cruisers, was prevented from getting in a shot at them by the work of the destroyers. Murphy continued to shadow them and at 0412, at first light, was able to send in detailed reports correctly identifying the two vessels. It was not long before the first Catalina from Midway homed on to the cruisers' position, she reported them as battleships. On Midway atoll the engines of the bombers began to burst into life and plane after plane began to roll down the airstrip and lift into the sky. The long ordeal of the *Mogami* and *Mikuma* was about to begin.

First of the American aircraft into the hunt were the Fortresses, eight of which took off at 0430. They failed to find their targets in the weather conditions then prevailing and aimlessly orbited Kure hoping for better information to reach them. When the PBY report of 'two battleships streaming oil', came in some hours later they moved out to try again.

But before they arrived, more positive action had been taken by the marine dive-bombers. Having lost two commanding officers the previous day *VMSB-241* was now led by Captain Marshall Tyler. Damage and losses had reduced this gallant force to only twelve combat-fit aircraft, six Vindicators and six

Dauntlesses. The weather was clear as they took off and headed out over the ocean at 0700.

Within forty-five minutes the marine bombers had located the long oil-slick of the damaged *Mikuma* and ran up it to their targets. They commenced their attacks at 0805.

First in were the older Vindicators using glide-bombing methods. But the two Japanese cruisers, although crippled in their hulls, had not had their armaments in any way damaged. They were crack ships and their gunners were both accurate and determined. A very heavy barrage met the Vindicators as they approached and the flak spoilt their aim. The sea boiled around the two ships but only near-misses were scored.

One of the Vindicators was caught in the flak bursts and caught fire. The pilot, Captain Richard E. Fleming USMC, could have had but seconds to realise that his aircraft was doomed. He managed to hold his blazing bomber steady at the *Mikuma* and attempted a suicide crash into her bridge. The heavy cruiser turning to meet the attack was able to prevent this but, at full speed and trailing smoke and flame, Fleming's aircraft ploughed straight into the ship's superimposed 'X' turret aft and blew up.

The burning gasoline from the pulverised Vindicator ignited the cordite of the turrets' ammunition, cremating the turret crew at their posts. The flames licked aft over 'Y' turret as well and to the air intakes of the starboard engine room. The sucked-in flames there caused the gases to explode wiping out the entire engine room complement. Her speed fell away as her fire-fighting teams battled to bring the flames under control. Gradually they mastered the blaze but now *both* heavy cruisers were cripples.

At 0830 as the dive-bombers winged their way back to Midway the eight B-17s arrived over the ships and made their high-level attacks, but again their bombs fell harmlessly into the water and two of the big bombers failed to return from this mission.

Throughout the long daylight hours of 5 June, and on through the night, the two cruisers painfully crawled away from Midway at twelve knots. For almost twenty-four hours they were allowed to continue their withdrawal unmolested. It seemed that, after all, they were to be spared.

Due to the uncertainty that prevailed on both sides that day, 5 June, was something of an anti-climax after the tremendous events of the 4th. Vast forces were still in motion across the whole battleground but contact was, more often than not, fleeting and unrewarding.

On the Japanese side the day was spent in the concentrating of all forces into one unified command under Yamamoto himself.

The main body had continued to steer east throughout the night and soon after dawn had rendezvoused with Admiral Kondo and his battleship and cruiser force some 320 miles north-west of Midway. Admiral Nagumo, with his band of cripples, should have also appeared but failed to do so. The combined battleship force then came about on a north-westerly course and the small carrier *Hosho* flew off air searches to locate him.

Nagumo was finally found by the aircraft at 0955 some forty miles away and soon these survivors had joined the main body and Kondo, to present a fleet of imposing appearance and strength. There was little however that Yamamoto could do with his force now that it was daylight, except continue to put more miles between it and the searching American carriers.

What of the *Hiryu*, which Nagumo was supposed to be escorting? She had in fact been left many miles astern, a battered and drifting shell. According to the reports of her destroyer escort she had long since slipped below the waves but around dawn came the remarkable news from one of *Hosho*'s search planes, that she was in fact, still very much afloat. Moreover signs of life were seen aboard her.

Admiral Nagumo therefore at once sent back the destroyer *Tanikaze* (Commander Motomi Katsumi), to rescue any survivors and to make absolutely certain that *Hiryu* was put down before she was captured as a battle trophy by the Americans.

Katsumi therefore took his little destroyer out of the screen and away from the comforting bulks of the heavy ships and shaped course to the east, one lone destroyer heading into the very jaws of the oncoming American fleet from which all his vast companions were fleeing. The *Tanikaze* had an unenviable mission but Katsumi and his crew were to prove during the course of that day that they were no mean fighters. They saw more of their enemy that day than Yamamoto and Kondo ever did.

Meanwhile Spruance and Fletcher were considering what best to do next. The sighting reports of the *Tambor* had been so vague that there was still the possibility to be considered that the Japanese invasion was going ahead as planned. The *Enterprise* and *Hornet* had reversed course at midnight and were steaming westward far north of Midway. But, on receipt of this first signal, Spruance swung round south-west to close the atoll and give the maximum air support he could to forestall or defeat any such landing.

He had reached a position some 160 miles north-east of Midway by 0600 but by this time his battle chart was becoming full for, in addition to the two heavy cruisers, now correctly identified for what they were, fresh reports from the Midway-based Catalinas brought news both of Yamamoto's concentration and also of the still-floating *Hiryu* closer to hand.

Which target to strike at? To any commander having witnessed the power of the carrier-based bomber over the last days there could only be one answer. If any Japanese carriers were afloat, even though damaged, they, Spruance reasoned, constituted the greatest daytime threat. Accordingly then, the whole power of the American task forces was concentrated on locating and destroying the *Hiryu*, the burning hulk of which had already defied attempts by the Japanese to sink it, and towards which the *Tanikaze* was now steaming at full speed to do the job for them, if allowed.

Thus this useless hulk drew off the main American striking power and gave the *Mogami* and *Mikuma* their respite, while the great force of battleships away to the north-west was also left undisturbed.

At 1500 that afternoon the *Enterprise* and the *Hornet* commenced flying off the massive waves of two bomber groups, one for search and one for attack. Altogether *Enterprise* put thirty-

151

two Dauntless dive-bombers up and *Hornet* a further twenty-six to complete this task. They flew out to the north-west under lowering skies, but found nothing but empty ocean. After completing their areas of search, without result, this great mass of fifty-eight aircraft set course back towards their carriers as evening drew on.

Back at Midway the damage done to the refuelling facilities by the Japanese air strike was still proving a crippling factor in the ability of the aircraft based there to assist. Laborious hand refuelling slowed their operations down to such an extent that only in the afternoon was a second wave of aircraft ready to take to the air, and these, eight B-17s, were sent out to locate the 'damaged Japanese carriers' as well.

They flew off to the north-west also and found nothing save the *Tanikaze* on her solitary mission.

The Japanese destroyer had been given the aid of a floatplane from the *Nagara* to help her to locate the wreck of the *Hiryu*. Despite this aircraft's searches, and her own diligent quartering of the area, the *Tanikaze* found no trace of the *Hiryu*. Nor was she ever seen again for it is now known that she finally sank around 0900 that morning, departing life unwitnessed and unmourned, save for a handful of survivors.

The B-17s therefore turned their attentions to *Tanikaze*, but the speeding destroyer was far too agile for altitude-bombing to have any effect and once more all the American bombs fell wide of the mark. Having survived this attack, and having found no trace of *Hiryu*, Katsumi put about to rejoin the main fleet. At 1636 however he sighted, and was sighted by, the dive-bombers from *Enterprise* and *Hornet*.

Over the next two hours the lone destroyer was subjected to continuous dive-bombing by almost the full weight of this air armada. The first attack was made by six SBDs and, at full helm and at her best speed, *Tanikaze* met the bombers with every gun she could muster. Twisting and turning, the destroyer was near-missed but she evaded every bomb aimed at her.

Next the destroyer came under attack from a larger group, no less than twenty-six dive-bombers concentrating on her, but again Katsumi brought his ship through this assault without damage, with his gunners managing to knock down one Dauntless with a direct hit of their own. It seemed a miracle, but they were not out of the wood yet. In screamed a new attack, the final one of the day, again by six dive-bombers. It was well pushed home and this time the *Tanikaze* did not escape without damage. A solitary near-miss exploded hard alongside X turret astern. Fragments of this bomb penetrated the gun house and ignited the cordite inside, killing the whole turret crew instantly. But this damage had no effect on the destroyer's speed or seaworthiness and that attack was the final one she had to undergo. The victorious destroyer rejoined Yamamoto just after dusk and was to be congratulated on a very valiant fight against heavy odds.

That *Tanikaze* survived the attacks of eight B-17s and no less than thirty-eight dive-bombers, although alone and unsupported, was an indication that the bomber was not yet quite the irresistible instrument of war that was claimed. But in the face of the devastation of the previous day's fighting, and in the ultimate fate of the *Mogami* and *Mikuma*, the fight of the *Tanikaze* was ignored and forgotten.

The SBDs finally returned to their carriers at the end of a frustrating day to find that night had fallen. The landing of aircraft on their carriers at night had not yet been attempted by the Americans in the war. With considerable courage the flyers accomplished it. In this way they were aided by the captains of the carriers themselves. Risking Japanese submarines the *Enterprise* switched on all her deck lights, and the *Hornet* blinked hers on and off. One by one, exhausted and with little fuel left in reserve for a second try, the SBDs glided in and bounced on to the decks. In the end almost every one of the fifty-seven made it, although, not surprisingly, five of *Hornet*'s bombers alighted on *Enterprise*, while *Hornet* took aboard one *Enterprise* Dauntless. Only one bomber was forced to ditch.

Spruance was reconsidering his policy. There was no sight of the enemy carriers, no invasion had manifested itself either and the heavy ships of the Japanese were still retiring to the west of him at good speed. Moreover he was still suspicious of a trap and he still refused to be lured too far. He considered the old maxim of a bird in the hand as being the most certain way of producing at least some positive results on the morrow, and so, accordingly, Kurita's two crippled cruisers were thus to be marked down for final elimination on the 6th. At 2040 therefore, *Enterprise*, *Hornet* and their escorts turned west once more to close the gap between them and their intended prey.

Yamamoto too was still vacillating between final and absolute acceptance of defeat and the temptation of trying to gain something positive from the battle to lessen the blow.

During the course of the day many burnt and injured survivors from the four big carriers were transferred from the destroyers to the better facilities of the battleships *Haruna*, *Kirishima*, *Mutsu* and *Nagato* where they could be better cared for. This operation was made in a heavy swell which called for careful and skilful ship handling and, in the end, despite the resulting risks, the fleet hove-to and the shuttle was completed by the ships' boats. It was a long job and night had fallen before it was fully completed.

On completion of this humanitarian task the combined force steered towards their refuelling point and out of range of all American aircraft. Dawn on 6 June found this great assembly some 600 miles from the tiny atoll they had sailed forth to conquer. All aboard were in sombre mood.

Away to the east another group of warships spent the day in comparative peace and isolation.

It will be recalled that the damaged *Yorktown*, abandoned by her ship's company, was listing alarmingly. It seemed a matter of hours before she too joined the four Japanese carriers on the seabed.

Admiral Fletcher with the *Astoria* and *Portland*, together with destroyers crammed with survivors, led off to the east and, at 1800, he sent back the destroyer *Hughes* to stand by the *Yorktown* and administer her death rites. The Americans, like the Japanese, were anxious that their crippled carrier should not be captured by enemy forces intact.

Accordingly the *Hughes* (Lieutenant Commander Donald J. Ramsey) maintained her vigil all through the night of the 4th-5th. At first light those aboard the destroyer watching the drifting carrier were amazed to see a burst of machine-gun fire from her into the water alongside. Those with glasses focused them on the spot and saw a sailor waving his arms to attract their attention. A boat was lowered and returned to the destroyer with two seamen, both of them in a bad way. One had a fractured skull and the other severe abdominal wounds. It transpired that when the bulk of the 2270-man crew of the *Yorktown* hastily took to the water those unfortunates were left in the sick bay to their fate. Such callousness seems hard to credit but such are the facts. One of the seriously wounded men had, by heroic efforts, managed to drag himself up on to the tilting deck and fire the guns which brought their rescue.

Unfortunately his brave sacrifice was not fully rewarded for, although it saved the life of his companion, his exertions proved too much for him and he died shortly after aboard the *Hughes*.

Lieutenant Commander Ramsey therefore sent a small salvage party back to the carrier to ensure that no others were similarly abandoned and they found that secret documents had not been deposited over the side in weighted bags as they should have been and that coding machines had been left aboard intact!

As a result of this examination Ramsey was able to signal to Fletcher that, in his opinion, the *Yorktown* was perfectly capable of being salvaged. While this search was in progress another remarkable rescue was made by the *Hughes*, that of one of the *Yorktown*'s fighter pilots. He had had his Wildcat shot down the day before and had been given up for lost. However he had managed to ditch, clamber aboard his inflatable dinghy and, when dawn broke revealing his old ship on the horizon, had rowed the six miles towards her!

On receipt of the news of the *Yorktown* Admiral Nimitz back at Pearl Harbor at once sailed the salvage tug *Navajo* up from French Frigate Shoals to effect a salvage of this valuable vessel. The destroyer *Gwin* (Commander John M. Higgins) had also been despatched post-haste from Pearl earlier, to reinforce Spruance, and Nimitz diverted her to the area also to help *Hughes*.

By 1426 the *Vireo* had got a line aboard the *Yorktown* and was struggling to get her moving to the east but to little avail;

the deadweight of the listing carrier proving more than a single tug could manage, especially against the prevailing headwinds.

When *Gwin* arrived with Commander Holcomb aboard he took over salvage efforts and sent over a second team from the destroyer to assist those from *Hughes*, but little could be done before nightfall. At dusk *Yorktown* had hardly moved at all and still lay over at an alarming 25 degrees to port. The admiral remained some 150 miles east of her, transferring survivors from his destroyers to his two cruisers and refuelling, and took no part in the rescue operation with his two big ships that day until the afternoon.

It was then decided by Admiral Fletcher and Captain Buckmaster that a proper salvage attempt should be made and a party of 170 volunteers was transferred to the destroyer *Hammann* (Commander Arnold E. True). Meanwhile the destroyer *Monaghan* (Lieutenant Commander William P. Burford), had been sent off to further assist *Hughes* and *Gwin*.

At 0200 on 6 June the *Hammann*, escorted by the destroyers *Balch* and *Benham*, found this group of three destroyers and a tug with *Yorktown* in tow, still struggling to gain headway. At dawn the *Hammann* had lashed herself alongside the carrier while the other five destroyers circled out to provide air and underwater protection. Using *Hammann* as their floating base, this new team set to work with a will to a well-prepared plan of action under the direction of Captain Buckmaster.

The still-smouldering fire in her rag stowage was put out immediately, all aircraft remaining aboard the carrier were dumped, without ceremony, over the side to lighten the ship, along with everything movable on the port side.

Counterflooding was carried out to reduce the ship's list and by noon it seemed as if their efforts were to be crowned with success, and that, for the second time in a month, the old *Yorktown* would come back from the grave.

For *Yorktown* the dawn of 6 June brought high hopes of salvation; that same sunrise brought only the promise of nemesis to the two crippled Japanese cruisers dragging their wounded bulks through the dark waters far to the south-west.

Already search planes were in the air from Spruance's carriers and soon found them. At 0800 the first attack wave was flying off the *Hornet*, twenty-six Dauntless bombers escorted by eight Wildcats. These were followed at 1045 by a second wave from the *Enterprise*, thirty-one dive-bombers, the three remaining Devastator torpedo-bombers and an escort of twelve Wildcats. Following up this mass of aircraft was a third strike, again launched from *Hornet*, of twenty-four SBDs and eight fighters.

Nor was this all for, from Midway, the B-17s were now ready for yet another attempt, having been reinforced from Oahu. Two dozen Fortresses were therefore despatched by Captain Simard to join in the assault.

The weather that morning had improved vastly over the previous day with light airs and sunlight. Steaming at high speed between strikes, the American carriers were able to launch straight into the wind without deviating from their course and rapidly closed the gap that the damaged heavy cruisers had attempted to open up the previous day. By midday the two forces were less than ninety miles apart and the American airmen were for the first time able to see both forces at the same time in the clear conditions.

Without any hope of air cover the two Japanese heavy cruisers had to rely totally on their own guns, and those of their two escorting destroyers, to defend themselves against this mass of aircraft. The contest was made even more uneven in that both Japanese vessels could only respond sluggishly to helm orders. In effect they had to sit and take it. They were to prove just how tough they were during the ensuing hours.

The first wave reached their target at 0950 and split their attacks between both cruisers. Heavy and accurate flak rose up to meet them as they commenced their dives and one of the bombers was hit fair and square and crashed like a torch into the ocean. But the other dive-bombers bore on through it all to drop their bombs all around the two cripples. They soon started taking direct hits.

Mogami was struck twice. One bomb pierced the armoured top of an 8in gun turret, slicing through the metal like a tin-opener and detonating inside with fearful carnage. A second bomb burst directly on the amidships torpedo tubes and smashed down into the decks below starting fierce fires. Amidst the shattered compartments filled with smoke and mounds of

157

dead and wounded men, the fire fighting teams fought heroically to stem the advance of the flames.

Mikuma fared worse though, taking three direct hits which reduced her upperworks to a shambles and smashed enormous holes through her hull sides from which smoke belched and broken steam pipes hissed and blew. Despite this both cruisers kept their speed. Three bombers were claimed shot down.

The second wave of American aircraft now arrived from the *Enterprise*. They had initially been misled by a report from the *Hornet* group that a damaged battleship was forty miles to the north of the heavy cruisers, but in fact this was a mis-sighting of the same group, and, after failing to locate this mythical battlewagon, the *Enterprise* aircraft, led by Lieutenant Short, turned their full attention to the cruisers. The flak was weaker now and it was all too easy.

Almost at once the *Mikuma* took two heavy bombs, one just forward of the bridge and the other amidships, both of which opened her 'tweendecks up and started enormous fires. Men below were scythed down in heaps while trying to fight these fires, when three more direct hits smashed into her tortured upperworks, reducing them to a pitted, smoking pile of debris. Her guns cocked and askew, her torpedo tubes trailing in the sea like the entrails of a wounded animal, the *Mikuma* slowed to a standstill, ablaze from stem to stern.

Her captain, Captain Shakao Sakiyama, ordered abandon ship and called the destroyer *Arashio* alongside to assist in this, but the terrible fires issuing from the rent and riven hull drove her back. Her surviving crew members took to the water from her quarterdeck in their hundreds and swam over to the destroyer. As the Wildcat fighters zoomed in, machine-gunning the wounded huddled around her wrecked superstructure and burnt-out gun turrets, the American pilots could clearly see the helpless men shaking their fists at them in impotent rage and despair.

But there was no mercy. The American pilots had the blood lust now and still remembered Pearl Harbor. As the *Arashio* pulled away with her decks packed solid with survivors and badly burned wounded she was attacked by the third wave of dive-bombers from the *Hornet*. A bomb smashed her after deck

158

and burst right in the middle of one such densely packed group. It was a scene of ultimate horror.

The *Mogami* was hit again in this attack, the bomb penetrating through her lower decks and sealing up the surviving engine-room where some ninety men were roasted alive in a matter of minutes when one of the fuel burners was jammed open by the blast. The destruction below decks, as above, defied description, but despite this, the crew fought on and by some miracle not only managed to bring these devastating fires under control, but were able to shore up the twisted and buckled bulkheads, stop the inrush of water through the warped and twisted plates of the hull and maintain their ship, little more than a floating scrapyard, on a course to safety. Amazingly the *Mogami* survived this merciless battering and came home safely to Truk. She would fight again.

Not so her equally resilient sister. The inside of the ship now resembled a furnace and soon an enormous internal hammer blow shook her battered hull as a magazine blew up. It was the end. Captain Sakiyama had been badly wounded in the third attack but stayed in command until she sank. He was picked up by the destroyers and transferred later to the cruiser *Suzuya* where he died on the 13th.

Thus died the *Mikuma*.

The two destroyers survived, although both of them were hit by one bomb each, the *Arashio* losing Commander Ogawa, the divisional commander and thirty-seven men, while *Asashio* lost twenty-two men. Each destroyer claimed to have shot down one bomber during the attacks and their hulls and engines remained sound as they escorted the *Mogami* to safety. She had been hit a total of six times and lost nine officers and eighty-one men, which, in view of the punishment she took, was remarkably light. Although *Mikuma* did not finally sink until that night, some 1000 men accompanied her to her last resting place.

It remained for the Air Force to provide the only comic relief for this day of carnage and death. As usual the B-17s thundered into the clear sky in search of the two cruisers, full of confidence and dash but, yet again, failed to find them all. Only too aware of just how much they had failed to justify the enormous amount of pre-war confidence in the heavy bomber as the ultimate weapon against warships, they cast about them in desperation for an enemy ship to attack.

Six of the Forts finally found something that afternoon. A vessel was seen far below and was unhesitatingly identified as a cruiser. Here was the enemy! In steady formation the six great planes made their runs over the target and released their loads. Down sailed their giant bombloads towards the enemy to burst all around their target which disappeared immediately in a welter of smoke and spray. It was as simple as they had always claimed it would be. So much for seapower. The Forts landed back at their base to claim that they had sunk a Japanese cruiser in the incredible time of fifteen seconds! It was not until a few days later that the American submarine *Grayling* returned to port and the truth came out. The Japanese cruiser attacked by the B-17s was in fact the *Grayling* and the reason she had disappeared so quickly was that she had crash-dived on being bombed by 'friendly' aircraft. Her commanding officer enquired why this had happened; the Army Air Force tried to pretend that it hadn't!

As the reports of the air strikes on the cruisers came in to *Yamato*'s bridge Admiral Yamamoto decided on one last ploy to bring the American task force to action. First he made up a cruiser striking force and despatched it to the aid of *Mogami* and *Mikuma.* This comprised the heavy cruisers *Atago, Chokai, Chikuma, Kumano, Suzuya* and *Tone*, the light cruiser *Jintsu* and the destroyers of her division, eight in all. The Kondo force and the main body also steered south in support.

If the Americans could be persuaded to sail on, the much-cherished, much-discussed and much-abandoned night surface action could yet take place. If not, perhaps the scratch force of 100 aircraft from *Hosho* and *Zuiho* and the cruisers could be supplemented by air strikes from Wake Island itself to provide the necessary air strength for a dawn action on the 7th. Some fifty medium bombers were stationed there awaiting just such an eventuality. Such was the thinking on *Yamato* that evening and accordingly Yamamoto issued orders at 1800 to that effect. His whole great fleet moved south during the night in readiness.

160

It was merely wishful thinking.

Admiral Spruance had not been tempted on the night of 4th-5th to indulge in such folly, nor had he taken a chance on the night of the 5th-6th. It was not likely therefore that he would jeopardise his obvious victory at this late hour by playing the Japanese game. Nor did he.

The returning American aircrews landed on their carriers at the end of their resources for the time being. There is no doubt that had they have been called upon to go yet again they would have done so eagerly, but Spruance considered that they had dulled the edge of their staying power after three days of exhausting action.

In addition, oil problems were beginning to affect his fleet, and, after the redeployment of several of his destroyers to aid *Yorktown*, refuel, and rescue ditched aviators, he found himself with only four destroyers, *Aylwin*, *Conyngham*, *Ellet* and *Phelps*, to provide an anti-submarine escort for his two carriers and six cruisers. It was plainly insufficient and the risk of running into a concentration of Japanese submarines were equally as great as that of heading into the arms of the Japanese battle-ships or the Wake Island bombers.

Admiral Spruance was now 400 miles west of Midway but that was his deepest penetration into what was still very much a Japanese lake. The American ships came about and headed in search of the refuelling tankers *Cimarron* and *Guadalupe*.

From all that vast array of ships and admirals that comprised the Japanese fleet it fell upon one small vessel and one very junior officer to wring from the battle the one scrap of comfort allowed to them. The ship was the submarine *I-168*, the man was Tanabe.

After the rather farcical demonstration against Midway the previous night, Tanabe had cast about him to the north of the atoll seeking the crippled carrier. The ocean was large and his submarine but a tiny speck upon it and it seemed like a very long shot indeed that he might come across her. But as he had shown before during this battle Tanabe was nothing if not patient and determined. For long hours his tiny craft scoured the wide waters until, at 1300 on the afternoon of the 7th, he was to succeed.

Into his sights appeared the listing *Yorktown*, her decks alive with activity, the *Hammann* still alongside and, in a wide screen around her, the deadly forms of five American destroyers.

Undeterred by the odds against him as usual, Tanabe shaped course for his attack. He penetrated to within 1900 yards of the carrier. At 1330 he fired a careful and precise salvo of four torpedoes, ascertained that they were running 'straight and true', and then, and only then, took *I-168* down in a deep dive.

The effect of his salvo was shattering. Although one torpedo sped wide of the target, the other three were right on target. These deadly missiles were seen approaching by the crew of the *Hammann*. The machine-gunners opened up on them in a vain attempt to detonate them in the water and Commander True up on the bridge ordered full speed astern on his inboard engine. As they watched in the last fleeting seconds the first torpedo disappeared beneath the destroyer in the vicinity of 'B' gun and struck home on the *Yorktown* with a deafening explosion. Almost instantly the second torpedo passed beneath the *Hammann* and hit the carrier with 'a deep bellying roar'.

All aboard the *Hammann* were flung on their faces by the blast but almost at the same instant the third torpedo, running shallow, struck the destroyer herself. It penetrated the number two fire-room and exploded with such enormous violence that it broke the destroyer's back instantly.

In a shower of oil, water and flying debris the *Hammann* began to settle rapidly in two halves and True ordered abandon ship. True had suffered a broken rib from the blasts and was later picked up out of the water some four hours later by the *Balch* after supporting in the water two seamen, both of whom were found to be dead when picked up.

The hero of the ship was Torpedoman First-Class Berlyn Kimbrel. Although the *Hammann* went down in only four minutes Kimbrel was able in that brief time to check that all depth-charges were set to 'safe' and pass out lifebelts to his comrades on the quarterdeck. He was the last to leave the ship. Despite his efforts he and a great many other survivors in the water were killed by an underwater explosion that ripped the sinking ship apart as she went down. This explosion was probably caused by one of her own torpedo warheads exploding as one fish was seen 'running hot' in its tube as the ship went down. Out of her total complement of thirteen officers and 228 men more than eighty were killed by these explosions or died of their injuries aboard the rescue destroyers.

The two torpedoes that hit *Yorktown* exploded just above her bilge keel and the shock forced her away from the sinking destroyer, and all the loose gear, including a couple of aircraft and the survivors' personal effects, fell into the sea. However as these hits were on the opposite side to the earlier ones the immediate effect was to reduce her list to about 17 degrees. But she was filling with water faster than the pumps could deal with. The tug *Vireo* cut her towline and embarked all the salvage crew and transferred them to the destroyer *Benham*.

Meanwhile the boats of the escorting squadron, *Gwin*, *Hughes*, *Benham*, *Monaghan* and *Balch*, were conducting a high pressure hunt for *Yorktown*'s assailant. As Morison stated all these ships were veterans from North Atlantic waters where submarines constituted the main enemy. It was something of a blow to their pride that *I–168* had been able to penetrate their defences so easily and they were determined on vengeance.

Depth-charges rained down, Tanabe counting no less than sixty near-misses. The Japanese submarine trembled under the hammer blows of such a concentration and eventually the hull was so strained that Tanabe had no choice but to bring his boat to the surface and hope to fight it out or at least allow his crew to escape certain death.

But when *I–168* did surface the sea was empty, the hunters had lost the scent and had returned to the *Yorktown* to rescue destroyer *Hammann*'s survivors. *I–168* was reprieved and, at slow speed, Tanabe steered away from the area. His boat survived to bring news of the only real success the Japanese enjoyed on the field of Midway.

The *Yorktown* continued to settle firmly although Captain Buckmaster was still determined to reboard and make further attempts at salvaging. This he planned to do at dawn. But after several hours, with the sky growing lighter, the great ship suddenly lurched over to port and they knew she was doomed.

163

The final scene was a fitting one for this veteran carrier who had given her all in two major fights. The escorting destroyers huddled around her, powerless now to aid her, and they half-masted their colours. Their decks were lined with silent watchers standing at attention, some saluting in farewell.

The end came at 0600 when, with a final lurch, her loose equipment crashing and smashing around inside her empty hull, the *Yorktown* rolled over and went swiftly down to her last resting place, 2000 fathoms below the waters she had contested and won so well. Only one final act in that great drama remained to be played out before the final curtain.

By dawn of 7 June Admiral Yamamoto had finally thrown in the towel. It was a hard decision for him to make and the whole of his staff shared their leader's vexation. Consequently much heart searching had taken place during the night before they bowed to the inevitable.

Yamamoto's last order had been issued the previous afternoon and had proclaimed stoutly that, in pursuance of a new battle plan, the combined fleet ' . . . will catch and destroy the enemy task force within attack range of air forces based on Wake Island'.

Yamamoto's outward confidence thus reflected in this uncompromising signal was not however matched by his real inner feelings. He must have known that it was all over. The fact that he was really resigned to his defeat can be seen in a remark attributed to him as early as the 5th, during a prolonged discussion on his flag deck on a suggested withdrawal. How, it was asked, could such a defeat be explained to the Emperor? Japan had not been defeated in battle for centuries.

'Leave that to me,' Yamamoto is said to have exclaimed angrily, 'I am the only one who must apologise to His Majesty for this defeat.'

Although Admiral Nagumo's errors of judgement on the 4th had placed his commander-in-chief in this unenviable position, was it not possible for the brilliant commander of the combined fleet to rectify the situation even at this late stage? It was certainly expected of him even though the general verdict of history is that it was already too late for him to save the day, and his cherished plan.

Fuchida and Okumiya hold this view, that the defeat of the Japanese was all but fully completed before Yamamoto could bring his judgement to bear one way or another. Likewise Yamamoto's biographer was to claim a more embracing alibi: 'In the last analysis Yamamoto was not lucky.'

Arrogance, bad luck, and bad judgement in keeping Nagumo as his carrier commander before the battle commenced, lost Yamamoto the battle, was his judgement.

But as supreme commander on the spot, and unhindered by his superiors at home, Yamamoto had a duty to make a decision, and make it quickly. Instead he vacillated for three days. In so doing was he not committing *exactly* the same mistakes as Nagumo had done in as many hours of more concentrated action?

The answer must be yes. All discussion aboard the *Yamato* produced only increasingly desperate and unrealistic schemes. All the resolute orders issued achieved absolutely nothing positive to remedy the situation. The greatest fleet Japan had assembled in her history marched, and counter-marched around an empty sea some three hundred miles from its weaker enemy for three days without once glimpsing its opponents.

In the end Yamamoto's mind was made up for him. Not by a sudden, blinding stroke of inspiration, not by a careful reasoned and skilfully worked-out solution, but simply by a prosaic fact of logistics. In simple terms he had used up in useless meanderings all his fuel and now had no choice but to retire. All his flailing at empty air had merely used up his vital oil supplies and left him with no other option but to retreat.

The cruiser striking force had contacted the crippled *Mogami* and had commenced to escort her back to Truk, but of the Americans there had been no sign. Yamamoto had been outthought by Spruance. The huge bows of the battleships of the main body therefore turned away from Midway for the last time at 0700 that morning and headed towards their final refuelling rendezvous in order to top up with sufficient fuel to start on their long, long voyage back to the Inland Sea.

At home the enormous significance of the defeat did not at first sink in. Tokyo radio was announcing a glorious Japanese victory with heavy US losses. The dispirited men aboard the returning ships, laden with horribly burnt and wounded men, knew the real truth and were disgusted at the misrepresentation. After a little while this feeling got back to Japan also and the radio became muted on the Midway operation, concentrating all the accolades on the minor triumphs in the Aleutians. By the time the Japanese fleet got back to the home waters, a tight security clamp-down was in force. The returning Japanese sailors were treated more as lepers than fighting men who had done their best in honourable combat. All references to the battle were forbidden.

It was a bitter homecoming.

CHAPTER SEVEN

A FAMOUS VICTORY

Midway was, without a doubt, one of the most decisive sea battles in history. It could also be claimed that it was one of the most complete victories achieved by any combatant, on land, sea or in the air, during World War II. That the battle was a confusing one typifies air/sea warfare as it had then developed. In the way the battle was planned and fought it was classic. The methods of fighting such a battle were largely experimental which helped to create a confused evaluation of it. The fact that it was also fought across the International Date Line did nothing to simplify the researchers seeking to define its new category in history.

It was first and foremost a battle that could, in the end, have gone either way simply because of its novelty and complexity. Despite the apparently overwhelming might of the Japanese on paper the fruits of victory went to the Americans, but a handful more fighters on one side, a little less luck on the other, and Midway could have quickly become the decisive Japanese triumph that they had both planned for and expected.

Although then Midway turned out to be a complete and undisputed American victory there can be no single clear reason for the result turning out the way it did. Let us therefore examine briefly each factor that weighed in the balance which finally tipped towards Fletcher and Spruance and away from Yamamoto and Nagumo.

First the basic plan as drawn up by the Japanese. It was, as we have seen, largely the work and design of Admiral Yamamoto himself. It was he who saw the need for such a battle, he who selected the target and he who held out for his choice against all counter-argument. Can the plan itself be held up as the reason for the Japanese defeat?

Here I think not. There can be little doubt that Admiral Yamamoto was absolutely correct in his selection of Midway as the principal target, bearing in mind that the occupation of the atoll itself was always, in his mind, merely the means to an end. That end was to lure out what remained of the Americans' sea-power in the Pacific, draw it into waters of Japan's own choosing and there confront it with overwhelming strength in order to crush it absolutely.

He was opposed in this choice of target on the grounds that Midway, if won, could not be held for long without causing a serious drain on Japan's resources. In addition there appeared to be far more worthwhile objectives down in the south-western Pacific. A drive through the Solomons and onwards would sever links between America and Australia. All this was true but Yamamoto was far more long-sighted in his view. If, as he wished, the United States fleet, and especially her remaining aircraft-carriers, could be knocked out once and for all, all these other glittering prizes would fall into Japan's lap anyway with very little further effort. American sea-power held the key to a Japanese victory. It would make little odds, and in the event it did not, how many islands Japan took if the American fleet was still active and could retake them at a future date .

Admiral Yamamoto certainly could better appreciate the potential strength of America than could his contemporaries and seniors. He was aware that the vast industrial strength of that nation was even then in the process of constructing a fleet of such size and magnitude than anything seen afloat in any ocean before, would be dwarfed by comparison with it. Yamamoto held firmly to the creed that the only way in which this mighty assembly could be held at arm's length from Japan itself was for his nation to gain an overwhelming and undisputed hold of the Pacific, while there was still time, so that the Americans' new fleets, when they eventually came to fruition, would be faced with the most daunting task imaginable.

Should his ultimate objective have been achieved at Midway then this ambition was at least possible, for then not only

Hawaii and the south-west approaches to Australia would have lain completely unprotected against any moves Japan might have wished to make, but the whole western seaboard of the United States would have been exposed to anything his fleet cared to do.

Although talk of carrier attacks and shore bombardments of Seattle, Portland, San Francisco, San Diego and control of the vital Panama Canal may now seem like merely the unattainable dreams of romantic fantasy by the Japanese, had the three American carriers been destroyed, as hoped, and the losses to the Japanese fleet held to acceptable limits, then all that stood in Yamamoto's way were a few ancient battleships and some submarines.

On a grander scale was the realisation that such ultimate hopes *could* effectively seal off the Pacific Ocean to the Western powers while an attack from the other side via the Indian Ocean would have to penetrate the barriers of the Burmese and Malayan jungles and the crescent of the newly established bases in the Dutch East Indies. It would seem therefore that Yamamoto's plan offered the Japanese the only, albeit slender, hope they had of concluding a victorious peace.

It is when the actual organisation of the Japanese task forces in readiness for the battle is examined that Admiral Yamamoto can be faulted. The battle had to be decisive and yet, as we have seen, the Japanese dispositions made it certain that it was not, at least for them. Even without the benefit of hindsight the fact that the Japanese commander-in-chief had spread his overwhelmingly superior forces out over so wide an area, thus making it impossible for them to support each other in any way, seems inexplicable.

The battle was ultimately decided by three American carriers opposed by four Japanese carriers, and yet Japan had eight carriers deployed in the operation. The fact that the other four were acting in subsidiary rôles, hundreds of miles from the vital battle area, meant, in fact, that they might just as well have stayed in port for all the good they did. Worse, a further two carriers could have been got ready but were left behind. So against the three American carriers the Japanese *could* have actually deployed *ten* which would have surely ensured the absolute victory they so badly wanted.

In the same manner the eleven battleships were also wasted by being split up in a similar fashion. Even the three largest, those retained by Yamamoto alone, could have tipped the scales, had they been on the spot where they could *use* their guns instead of several hundreds of miles astern of the Nagumo force where they were impotent. Both Fletcher and Spruance feared the power of the eleven battleships and made damn certain they kept out of arm's reach of any of them. In this the Japanese were more obliging than anything the American admirals could have hoped for. Like the four small carriers, the eleven mighty battleships might just as well have not been there at all in the way they were used.

Why is this so? The answer lies in over-confidence. In the grand design, all these forces (or at least most of them) *would* have achieved a fighting concentration in their own good time. Only after Midway had been occupied would all Yamamoto's great fleet gather together for the kill, for only *then*, or so they confidently assumed, would the American fleet respond and come running into the trap.

For the Japanese it was a tragic under-estimation of their opponent's intelligence system and the vital part this was to play. Even so, maximum strength at the decisive point of battle is the oldest concept of warfare and Yamamoto ignored it, to his ultimate cost.

Could faulty dispositions have been rectified by other factors once the battle was joined? Only by luck. Courage and heroism is quite insufficient in modern warfare and anyway such attributes are so common to *both* sides that they cancel out. Luck is also arbitrary of course, perhaps the luckiest side won? Again no, luck had no favourites either, both sides benefited at various stages of the battle with good fortune and flukes of chance. Both sides had ample misfortune also.

Individual acts of great bravery and heroism were common on the Japanese side, as on the American, in a battle renowned for such acts. Also, ship for ship, the Japanese were the equals, maybe in many cases, like the Zero fighters, the superiors to their American equivalents. Had the battle developed on the lines envisaged by Yamamoto then these factors would have counted to be sure, but then again on the American side there were others factors, equally important, such as radar and good intelligence.

Technology was to win the war for America as much as heroism and the radar carried by the American ships gave them those vital minutes of extra warning against incoming Japanese air strikes that was denied to the Japanese. It made all the difference. The Japanese ships had no warning at all when the SBDs zoomed out of the cloud banks above them.

It is true then that the Americans had inferior aircraft, but it was of no avail to Nagumo that his Zero fighters were better fighting machines when, at the vital point in time, they were not in position to intercept the Dauntless dive-bombers.

For the Americans the victory at Midway was achieved by a better use of inferior numbers. The intelligence work was superb and gave them an initial edge that they never lost. Even so the hand they were dealt was still a poor one and faulty playing of their inferior cards could have cost them the battle. In fact they didn't put a foot wrong.

Out-gunned and out-numbered the American admirals had not hesitated to stand up to all the Japanese could throw at them and they were not overawed by the same factors that bore up their opponents. Despite the previous Japanese successes on all fronts, by this time *nobody* in the United States fleet was inclined to under-estimate the Japanese Navy (except the war correspondents) they took up the challenge with resolution and skill.

Both Admirals Fletcher and Spruance showed a natural ability and flair, a reading of the course of the battle, that was decisive. Although they were to attribute much of the victory to luck and the courage of their young pilots, it is certain that, by their own wisdom and restraint, they pulled off a master-stroke.

Contrast the dazed fumblings of Nagumo on 4 June, and the muddled orders for strikes and counter-strikes made by Yamamoto on the days that followed, with the skilful placings of the two American task groups by Fletcher and the refusal to be drawn into further traps by Spruance. Despite all the detailed planning by the Japanese it was the Americans who remained

171

in control of events throughout the battle rather than the attacking Japanese.

Courage there was of course, a-plenty, and the self-sacrifice of so many young men was a beacon to those that followed them in the long years of combat that followed. Waldron and his 'torpedo-eight', McClusky and Massey facing equally hopeless odds, the last dive of Captain Fleming, backed up by the persistence of Lieutenant Commander Brockman and doggedness of McClusky. In this battle proof was amply provided, had it ever been needed, that the American fighting man was the equal of any in the world.

Finally one must accept the Japanese verdict on their own failings as being equally the correct reason for the result of Midway. 'Victory disease' was how they described it, a feeling of invincibility that could not help but prevail after their unexpected chain of victories in the previous six months. They were *superior* to the Western nations at that point in time, had they not proved it time and time again? They were an élite force, and they were in overwhelming strength. They had pride, confidence and power. It is little wonder then that, being human, they became careless and the old saw, that pride cometh before a fall, has never been so crushingly given validity as on that bright day in June 1942.

One final speculation. What course would the war have taken had Yamamoto's dream come true? Would the dominance of the Imperial Japanese Navy have so over-awed the Americans that they would have become war-weary and thrown in the towel, not in total defeat, but in an acceptance of the *fait accompli*, leaving Japan with all her conquests and a free hand in Asia? Would the prospect of having to fight all the way back across the Pacific, with no battle fleet left with which to do it, have so sickened them that they would have accepted the 'Co-Prosperity' zone and all its ramifications? In the light of what happened it seems a superfluous question, but in the light of recent events in Vietnam and Angola it may not be so irrelevant after all. Was Yamamoto's final design based on an illusion of the American mind as fatally flawed as his Japanese opponents' views on the power of that great country?

In the author's opinion it was. It is unlikely that, even had the wildest dreams of the Japanese come to pass in 1942, it would have ended America's resolve to fight on to the bitter end. Yamamoto's ultimate hope was built on sand.

America, it is true, badly needed a victory. Their morale needed a boost and when they got it they were revitalised. But there would never have been any question of their quitting in 1942.

It is a fact that many Americans were jittery but the attack on Pearl Harbor had formed a strong and unified country behind the President, and he, at any rate, was absolutely determined on a crusade to the death against the expansion of dictatorships, as his later unilateral declaration of 'unconditional surrender', held by many to have prolonged the war, was to make obvious.

So, even had Midway been an American defeat instead of a victory, it is doubtful whether this would have made one jot of difference to the long-term morale of the people of the United States as a whole. Like the Japanese they were not used to being on the losing side, and their natural pride in their own country and the rightness of their cause had not yet been undermined by subversive elements and defeatists as in 1974. Left-wing students and communists alike could then be almost counted on one hand, they had not a fraction of the influence they hold today. In 1942, unlike 1974, there would certainly have been no wavering of purpose by the American nation.

A defeat at Midway may well have been regarded as an American Dunkirk, but it was not a Vietnam. The end result could not have lost the war for the United States but it would have made the winning of ultimate victory enormously more difficult than it eventually was, and that was tough enough.

And the battle itself? Much analysed and refought in books, its place in history is assured. One historian however has claimed that:

'Midway was the first and last gigantic carrier battle in the history of the world.'

In fact it was neither.

It was not the first, the Coral Sea battle can claim that distinction. It was not the last, by any means. The whole sub-

173

sequent three years of war in the Pacific was punctuated by similar clashes, the Eastern Solomons in August 1942, Santa Cruz in October of the same year and so on.

Midway was not in fact even the largest of such conflicts. At the Battle of the Philippine Sea in June 1944, a force of nine Japanese carriers sortied out and was met by twelve American carriers. In the resulting slaughter some three hundred Japanese aircraft were destroyed against thirty or so American planes. In addition three Japanese carriers were sunk.

What Midway was, in fact, was the most *important* of such carrier duels.

It did not mark, as has also been claimed, the demise of the Japanese Navy as a serious fighting force. Those who thought this suffered swift disillusionment off the island of Guadalcanal in the months that followed, when Japanese ships inflicted some stunning defeats upon American warships. Not until the huge battle of Leyte Gulf was that power finally destroyed, but that lay two years or more into the future.

What Midway *did* decide was that the seemingly irresistible tide of Japanese victory *could* be halted. The Japanese were beaten at their own game, and resoundingly beaten. Henceforth it was America, rather than Japan, who held the moral ascendancy, and, although Japan retained some initiative for a little longer, she was forced more and more to adopt a defensive posture. Such a course was entirely alien to her. And of course the development of the Pacific War more and more into a war of attrition could only end one way, as Yamamoto had foreseen.

In the history of sea warfare Midway was therefore a major milestone. For the United States Navy it was a coming of age, the real cornerstone of a fleet that hitherto had seen little major fighting. It was in fact the sound base on which the assumption of the mantle of the greatest sea-power on the globe was finally built. The trident passed across the Atlantic from Great Britain to the United States in 1942, and that position of awesome responsibility the Americans still hold, albeit falteringly now, to this day.

APPENDIX ONE

THE JAPANESE FORCES

COMBINED FLEET

Admiral Isoroku Yamamoto
   Chief of Staff: Rear Admiral Matome Ugaki

MAIN FORCE (First Fleet): Admiral Yamamoto

BATTLESHIP GROUP (Division 1): Admiral Yamamoto
   Yamato   Captain Gihachi Takayanagi (64,160 tons; 9 18in,
   12 6.1in, 12 5in guns; 28 knots)
   Nagato   Captain Hideo Yano
   Mutsu   Captain Teijiro Yamazumi (both 39,130 tons; 8
   16in, 18 5.5in, 8 5in guns; 25 knots)

CARRIER GROUP: Captain Kaoru Umetani
   Hosho   Captain Umetani (7470 tons; 8 bombers, Lieutenant
   Yoshiaki Irikiin; 25 knots)
   Yukaze   (Destroyer) Lieutenant Commander Shizuka Kaji-
   moto (Plane Guard Ship; 1215 tons; 4 4.7in guns; 6 21in
   torpedoes; 35 knots)

SPECIAL FORCE: Captain Kaku Harada (Seaplane Carriers
   with Midget Submarines embarked)
   Chiyoda   Captain Harada (11,020 tons; 12 midget subs; 29
   knots)
   Nisshin   Captain Katsumi Komazawa (11,317 tons; 12
   midget subs; 28 knots)

SCREEN (Destroyer Squadron 3): Rear Admiral Shintaro Hashimoto

Light Cruiser
  Sendai   Captain Nobue Morishita (5195 tons; 7 5.5in, 2 3in guns; 8 24in torpedoes; 35 knots)

Destroyer Division 11: Captain Kiichiro Shoji
  Fubuki   Commander Shizuo Yamashita
  Shirayuki   Commander Taro Sugahara
  Hatsuyuki   Lieutenant Commander Junnari Kamiura
  Murakumo   Commander Hideo Higashi

Destroyer Division 19: Captain Ranji Oe
  Isonami   Commander Ryokichi Sugama
  Uranami   Commander Tsutomu Hagio
  Shikinami   Commander Akifumi Kawahashi
  Ayanami   Commander Eiji Sakuma
    (All 2090 tons; 6 5in guns; 9 24in torpedoes; 34 knots)

1ST SUPPLY UNIT: Captain Shigeyasu Nishioka (Oilers)
  Naruto   Captain Nishioka (14,050 tons; 2 3in guns; 12 knots)
  Toei Maru
    (Mercantile conversion)

GUARD FORCE (Aleutians Screen): Vice Admiral Shiro Takasu

BATTLESHIP GROUP (Division 2): Vice Admiral Takasu
  Hyuga   Captain Chiaki Matsuda
  Ise   Captain Isamu Takeda (36,000 tons; 12 14in, 16 5.5in, 8 5in guns; 25 knots)
  Fuso   Captain Mitsuo Kinoshita
  Yamashiro   Captain Gunji Kogure (34,700 tons; 12 14in, 14 6in, 8 5in guns; 24 knots)

SCREEN: Rear Admiral Fukuki Kishi
Cruiser Division 9: Rear Admiral Kishi

Kitakami   Captain Saiji Norimitsu
Oi   Captain Shigeru Narita (5870 tons; 7 5.5in, 2 3in guns;
   8 24in torpedoes; 32 knots)

Destroyer Division 20: Captain Yuji Yamada
   Asagiri   Commander Nisaburo Maekawa
   Yugiri   Captain Masayoshi Motokura
   Shirakumo   Commander Toyoji Hitomi
   Amagiri   Captain Buichi Ashida (2090 tons; 6 5in guns; 9
   24in torpedoes; 34 knots)

Destroyer Division 24: Captain Yasuji Hirai
   Umikaze   Commander Nagahide Sugitani
   Yamakaze   Commander Shuichi Hamanaka
   Kawakaze   Commander Kazuo Wakabayashi
   Suzukaze   Commander Kazuo Shibayama (1580 tons; 5 5in
   guns; 8 24in torpedoes; 34 knots)

Destroyer Division 27: Captain Matake Yoshimura
   Ariake   Commander Shoichi Yoshida
   Yugure   Commander Kiyoshi Kamo
   Shigure   Commander Noboru Seo
   Shiratsuyu   Lieutenant Commander Kimmatsu Hashimoto
   (1715 tons; 5 5in guns; 6 24in torpedoes; 33 knots)

2ND SUPPLY UNIT: Captain Matsuo Eguchi (Oilers)
   San Clemente Maru   Captain Eguchi (5490 tons)
   Toa Maru (10,500 tons)

FIRST CARRIER STRIKING FORCE (First Air Fleet):
   Vice Admiral Chuichi Nagumo
   Chief of Staff: Rear Admiral Ryunosuke Kusaka

CARRIER GROUP: Vice Admiral Nagumo
Division 1: Vice Admiral Nagumo
   Akagi   Captain Taijiro Aoki (36,500 tons; 6 8in, 12 4.7in
   guns; 31 knots)

Air Unit embarked: Commander Mitsuo Fuchida
21 Zero fighters: Lieutenant Commander Shigeru Itaya
21 Val dive-bombers: Lieutenant Takehiko Chihaya
21 Kate torpedo-bombers: Lieutenant Commander Shigeharu Murata

Kaga Captain Jisaku Okada (38,200 tons; 10 8in, 16 5in guns; 28 knots)
Air Unit embarked: Lieutenant Commander Tadashi Kusumi
21 Zero fighters: Lieutenant Masao Sato
21 Val dive-bombers: Lieutenant Shoichi Ogawa
30 Kate torpedo-bombers: Lieutenant Ichiro Kitajima

Division 2: Rear Admiral Tamon Yamaguchi
Hiryu Captain Tomeo Kaku (15,900 tons; 12 5in guns; 34 knots)
Air Unit embarked: Lieutenant Joichi Tomonaga
21 Zero fighters: Lieutenant Shigero Mori
21 Val dive-bombers: Lieutenant Michio Kobayashi
21 Kate torpedo-bombers: Lieutenant Rokuro Kikuchi

Soryu Captain Ryusaku Yanagimoto (15,900 tons; 12 5in guns; 34 knots)
Air Unit embarked: Lieutenant Commander Takashige Egusa
21 Zero fighters: Lieutenant Masaharu Suganami
21 Val dive-bombers: Lieutenant Masahiro Ikeda
21 Kate torpedo-bombers: Lieutenant Heijiro Abe

SUPPORT GROUP: Rear Admiral Hiroaki Abe
Cruiser Division 8: Rear Admiral Abe
Tone Captain Tametsugu Okada
Chikuma Captain Keizo Komura (11,215 tons; 8 8in, 8 5in guns; 12 24in torpedoes; 35 knots)

2nd Section, Battleship Division 3: Captain Tamotsu Koma
Haruna Captain Koma
Kirishima Captain Keizo Komura (31,800 tons; 8 14in, 14 6in, 8 5in guns; 30 knots)

(Destroyer Squadron 10): Rear Admiral Susumu Kimura

Light Cruiser
  Nagara Captain Toshio Naoi (5170 tons; 7 5.5in, 2 3in guns; 8 24in torpedoes; 36 knots)

Destroyer Division 4: Captain Kosaku Ariga
  Nowaki Commander Magotaro Koga
  Arashi Commander Yasumasa Watanabe (Both 2030 tons; 6 5in guns; 8 24in torpedoes; 35 knots)
  Hagikaze Commander Juichi Iwagami
  Maikaze Commander Seiji Nakasugi (Both 2035 tons; 6 5in guns; 8 24in torpedoes; 35 knots)

Destroyer Division 10: Captain Toshio Abe
  Kazagumo Commander Masayoshi Yoshida
  Yugumo Commander Shigeo Semba
  Makigumo Commander Isamu Fujita (2070 tons; 6 5in guns; 8 24in torpedoes; 35 knots)

Destroyer Division 17: Captain Masayuki Kitamura
  Urakaze Commander Nagayoshi Shiraishi
  Isokaze Commander Shunichi Toshima
  Tanikaze Commander Motomi Katsumi
  Hamakaze Commander Tsuneo Orita (2030 tons; 6 5in guns; 8 24in torpedoes; 35 knots)

SUPPLY GROUP: Captain Masanao Oto (Oilers)
  Kyokuto Maru Captain Oto (10,052 tons)
  Shinkoku Maru (9500 tons)
  Toho Maru (9980 tons)
  Nippon Maru (9970 tons)
  Kokuyo Maru (10,000 tons)
    (All mercantile conversions)

MIDWAY INVASION FORCE (Second Fleet):
  Vice Admiral Nobutake Kondo
  Chief of Staff: Rear Admiral Kazutaka Shiraishi

INVASION FORCE MAIN BODY: Vice Admiral Kondo

Cruiser Division 4: Vice Admiral Kondo
  Atago   Captain Matsuji Ijuin
  Chokai   Captain Mikio Hayakawa (13,160 tons; 10 8in, 8 5in guns; 16 24in torpedoes; 34 knots)
Cruiser Division 5: Vice Admiral Takeo Takagi
  Myoko   Captain Teruhiko Miyoshi
  Haguro   Captain Tomoichi Mori (13,400 tons; 10 8in, 8 5in guns; 16 24in torpedoes; 33 knots)
Battleship Division 3: Rear Admiral Guinichi Mikawa
  Kongo   Captain Tomiji Koyanagi
  Hiei   Captain Masao Nishida (31,700 tons; 8 14in, 14 6in, 8 5in guns; 30 knots)

SCREEN (DESTROYER SQUADRON 4): Rear Admiral Shoji Nishimura
Light Cruiser
  Yura   Captain Shiro Sato (5170 tons; 7 5.5in, 2 3in guns; 8 24in torpedoes; 36 knots)
Destroyer Division 2: Captain Masao Tachibana
  Murasame   Commander Naoji Suenaga
  Samidare   Commander Takisaburo Matsubara
  Harusame   Commander Masao Kamiyama
  Yudachi   Commander Kiyoshi Kikkawa (1580 tons; 5 5in guns; 8 24in torpedoes; 34 knots)
Destroyer Division 9: Captain Yasuo Sato
  Asagumo   Commander Toru Iwahashi
  Minegumo   Commander Yasuatsu Suzuki
  Natsugumo   Commander Moritaro Tsukamoto (1960 tons; 6 5in guns; 8 24in torpedoes; 35 knots)

CARRIER GROUP: Captain Sueo Obayashi
  Zuiho   Captain Obayashi (11,260 tons; 8 5in guns; 28 knots)
    Air Unit embarked
      12 Zero fighters: Lieutenant Moriyasu Hidaka
      12 Kate torpedo-bombers: Lieutenant Kaji Matsuo
Destroyer
  Mikazuki   Lieutenant Commander Saneho Maeda (1310 tons; 4 4.7in guns; 6 24in torpedoes; 37 knots)

SUPPLY GROUP: Captain Jiro Murao
Oilers
  Sata Captain Murao (14,050 tons; 2 3in guns; 12 knots)
  Tsurumi Captain Toshizo Fujita (14,050 tons; 2 3in guns; 12 knots)
  Genyo Maru (10,020 tons)
  Kenyo Maru (9500 tons)
Repair Ship
  Akashi Captain Tsunekichi Fukuzawa (9000 tons; 4 5in guns; 19 knots)

CLOSE SUPPORT GROUP: Rear Admiral Takeo Kurita
Cruiser Division 7: Vice Admiral Kurita
  Kumano Captain Kikumatsu Tanaka
  Suzuya Captain Masatomi Kimura
  Mikuma Captain Shakao Sakiyama
  Mogami Captain Akira Soji (12,400 tons; 10 8in, 8 5in guns; 12 24in torpedoes; 34 knots)
Destroyer Division 8: Commander Nobuki Ogawa
  Asashio Commander Goro Yoshii
  Arashio Commander Hideo Kuboki (1960 tons; 6 5in guns; 8 24in torpedoes; 35 knots)
Oiler
  Nichiei Maru (7600 tons)

TRANSPORT GROUP: Rear Admiral Raizo Tanaka
  Captain Minoru Ota in command of the Midway Landing Force
Transports
  Kiyozumi Maru
  Zenyo Maru
  No 2 Toa Maru
  Argentina Maru
  Brazil Maru
  Azuma Maru
  Keiyo Maru
  Goshu Maru
  Kano Maru
  Hokuriku Maru

Kirishima Maru

Nankai Maru

Patrol Boats

No 1

No 2 (Converted destroyers used as fast transports; 1390 tons; 2 4.7in guns; 250 troops; 20 knots)

No 34 (935 tons; 2 4.7in guns; 150 troops; 18 knots)

Oiler

Akebono Maru

ESCORT (DESTROYER SQUADRON 2): Rear Admiral Tanaka

Light Cruiser

Jintsu Captain Torazo Kozai (5190 tons; 7 5.5in, 2 3in guns; 8 24in torpedoes; 35 knots)

Destroyer Division 15: Captain Shiro Sato

Kuroshio Commander Tamaki Ugaki

Oyashio Commander Tokikichi Arima (2030 tons; 6 5in guns; 8 24in torpedoes; 35 knots)

Destroyer Division 16: Captain Shiro Shibuya

Yukikaze Commander Kenjiro Tobita

Amatsukaze Commander Tameichi Hara

Tokitsukaze Commander Giichiro Nakahara

Hatsukaze Commander Kameshiro Takahashi (2030 tons; 6 5in guns; 8 24in torpedoes; 35 knots)

Destroyer Division 18: Captain Yoshito Miyasaka

Shiranuhi Commander Jisuo Akasawa

Kagero Commander Minoru Yokoi (Both 1960 tons; 6 5in guns; 8 24in torpedoes; 35 knots)

Kasumi Commander Kiyoshi Tomura

Arare Commander Tomoe Ogata (Both 2030 tons; 6 5in guns; 8 24in torpedoes; 35 knots)

SEAPLANE TENDER GROUP: Rear Admiral Ruitaro Fujita

Chitose Captain Tarohachi Shinoda (11,020 tons; 4 5in guns; 20 knots)

Air Group embarked

16 seaplane fighters

4 seaplane scouts

Kamikawa Maru Captain Tarohachi Shinoda (6860 tons; 2 3in guns)
    Air Group embarked
        8 seaplane fighters
        4 seaplane scouts
Destroyer
  Hayashio Captain Kiyoshi Kaneda (2030 tons; 6 5in guns; 8 24in torpedoes; 35 knots)
Patrol Boat (fast transport)
  No 35 (935 tons; 150 troops; 18 knots)

MINESWEEPER GROUP: Captain Sadatomo Miyamoto
Minesweepers
  Tama Maru No 3
  Tama Maru No 5
  Shonan Maru No 7
  Shonan Maru No 8
    (All ex-mercantile conversions)
Subchasers
  No 16
  No 17
  No 18
    (All 485 tons; 1 3in gun; 16 knots)
Supply Ship
  Soya Commander Toshi Kubota (3800 tons; 1 3in gun; 12 knots; ammunition ship)
Cargo Ships
  Meiyo Maru
  Yamafuku Maru

ADVANCE (SUBMARINE) FORCE (Sixth Fleet)
  Vice Admiral Teruhisa Komatsu at Kwajalein
  Chief of Staff: Rear Admiral Hisashi Mito
Light Cruiser
  Katori Captain Noboru Owada (5890 tons; 4 5.5in, 2 5in guns; 4 21in torpedoes; 18 knots)
Submarine Squadron 3: Rear Admiral Chimaki Kono

Submarine Tender
  Rio de Janeiro Maru (9620 tons)
Submarine Division 19: Captain Ryojiro Ono
  I–156   Lieutenant Commander Katsuo Ohashi
  I–157   Lieutenant Commander Sakae Nakajima
  I–158   Lieutenant Commander Soshichi Kitamura
  I–159   Lieutenant Commander Tamori Yoshimatsu
    (1635 tons; 1 4.7in gun; 8 21in torpedoes; 20/8 knots)
Submarine Division 30: Captain Masao Teraoka
  I–162   Lieutenant Commander Takaichi Kinashi (1635 tons;
    1 4.7in gun; 6 21in torpedoes; 20/8 knots)
  I–165   Lieutenant Commander Takae Harada
  I–166   Commander Makio Tanaka (1575 tons; 1 3.9in gun;
    6 21in torpedoes; 20/8 knots)
Submarine Division 13: Captain Takeharu Miyazaki
  I–121   Lieutenant Commander Yasuo Fujimori
  I–122   Lieutenant Commander Sadatoshi Norita
  I–123   Lieutenant Commander Toshitake Ueno
    (1142 tons; 1 5.5in gun; 4 21in torpedoes; 14/7 knots)

SHORE BASED AIR GROUP FOR MIDWAY EXPEDITIONARY FORCE

    (Aircraft for Midway embarked in Carrier Striking Forces
    together with their ground crews, etc.)
    36 Zero fighters: Lieutenant Commander Mitsugu Kokufuda
    10 Betty bombers to fly in from Wake Island
     6 Flying-boats to fly in from Jaluit

24TH AIR FLOTILLA: Rear Admiral Minoru Maeda
    (at Kwajalein)
Chitose Air Group: Captain Fujiro Ohashi (at Kwajalein)
    36 Zero fighters
    36 Betty twin-engined torpedo-bombers
1st Air Group: Captain Samaji Inouye (at Aur and Wotje)
    36 Zero fighters
    36 Betty twin-engined torpedo-bombers
14th Air Group: Captain Daizo Nakajima (at Jaluit and Wotje)
    10 Mavis long-range flying boats
     8 Emily long-range flying-boats

APPENDIX TWO

THE AMERICAN FORCES

CARRIER STRIKING FORCE

Admiral Chester W. Nimitz, Commander-in-Chief

TASK GROUP 17: Rear Admiral Fletcher

CARRIER GROUP: Captain Elliott Buckmaster
   Yorktown   Captain Buckmaster (19,900 tons; 8 5in guns; 34 knots)
   Air Group embarked: Lieutenant Commander Oscar Peterson
      VF 3   25 Wildcat fighters: Lieutenant Commander John S. Thach
      VB 3   18 Dauntless dive-bombers: Lieutenant Commander Maxwell Leslie
      VS 5   19 Dauntless dive-bombers: Lieutenant Wallace C. Short, Jr
      VT 3   13 Devastator torpedo-bombers: Lieutenant Commander Lance E. Massey

CRUISER GROUP: Rear Admiral William W. Smith
   Astoria   Captain Francis W. Scanland
   Portland   Captain Laurance T. Du Bose (9900 tons; 9 8in, 8 5in guns; 32 knots)

SCREEN: Captain Gilbert C. Hoover
Destroyer Squadron 2
   Hammann   Commander Arnold E. True
   Hughes   Lieutenant Commander Donald J. Ramsey

Morris Commander Harry B. Jarrett

Anderson Lieutenant Commander John K. B. Ginder

Russell Lieutenant Commander Glenn R. Hartwig (1570 tons; 5 5in, 4 1in guns; 12 21in torpedoes; 38 knots)

Gwin Commander John M. Higgins (1620 tons; 5 5in guns; 10 21in torpedoes; 37 knots)

TASK FORCE 16: Rear Admiral Raymond A. Spruance

TASK FORCE 16 CARRIER GROUP: Captain George D. Murray
Carriers

Enterprise Captain Murray (19,900 tons; 8 5in guns; 34 knots)

Air Group embarked: Lieutenant Commander Clarence W. McClusky

VF 6 27 Wildcat fighters: Lieutenant James S. Gray

VB 6 19 Dauntless dive-bombers: Lieutenant Richard H. Best

VS 6 19 Dauntless dive-bombers: Lieutenant Wilmer E. Gallaher

VT 6 14 Devastator torpedo-bombers: Lieutenant Commander Eugene E. Lindsey

Hornet Captain Marc A. Mitscher (20,000 tons; 8 5in guns; 34 knots)

Air Group embarked: Commander Stanhope C. Ring

VF 8 27 Wildcat fighters: Lieutenant Commander Samuel G. Mitchell

VB 8 19 Dauntless dive-bombers: Lieutenant Commander Robert R. Johnson.

VS 8 18 Dauntless dive-bombers: Lieutenant Commander F. Rodee

VT 8 15 Devastator torpedo-bombers: Lieutenant Commander John C. Waldron

CRUISER GROUP: Rear Admiral Thomas C. Kinkaid
Heavy Cruisers

New Orleans Captain Walter S. DeLany

Minneapolis   Captain Frank J. Lowry

Vincennes   Captain Frederick L. Riefkohl (All 9900 tons; 9 8in, 8 5in guns; 32 knots)

Northampton   Captain William W. Chandler (9050 tons; 9 8in, 8 5in guns; 32 knots)

Pensacola   Captain Frank L. Lowe (9100 tons; 10 8in, 8 5in guns; 32 knots)

Anti-aircraft Cruiser

Atlanta   Captain Samuel P. Jenkins (6000 tons; 16 5in guns; 8 21in torpedoes; 32 knots)

SCREEN:

Destroyer Squadron I: Captain Alexander R. Early

Phelps   Lieutenant Commander Edward L. Beck (1850 tons; 8 5in guns; 8 21in torpedoes; 37 knots)

Worden   Lieutenant Commander William G. Pogue

Monaghan   Lieutenant Commander William P. Burford

Aylwin   Lieutenant Commander George R. Phelan (All 1395 tons; 5 5in guns; 8 21in torpedoes; 36 knots)

Destroyer Squadron 6: Captain Edward P. Sauer

Balch   Lieutenant Commander Harold H. Tiemroth (1850 tons; 8 5in guns; 8 21in torpedoes; 37 knots)

Conyngham   Lieutenant Commander Henry C. Daniel (1500 tons; 5 5in guns; 12 21in torpedoes; 36 knots)

Benham   Lieutenant Commander Joseph M. Worthington

Ellet   Lieutenant Commander Francis H. Gardner

Maury   Lieutenant Commander Gelzer L. Sims (1500 tons; 4 5in guns; 16 21in torpedoes; 36 knots)

Oiler Group

Cimarron   Commander Russell M. Ihrig

Platte   Captain Ralph H. Henkle (7250 tons; 1 5in, 4 3in guns; 18 knots)

Destroyers

Dewey   Lieutenant Commander C. F. Chillingworth, Jr (1395 tons; 5 5in guns; 8 21in torpedoes; 36 knots)

Monssen   Commander Roland N. Smoot (1620 tons; 5 5in guns; 10 21in torpedoes; 37 knots)

SUBMARINE FORCE
Rear Admiral Robert H. English, Pearl Harbor
Midway Patrol Group
  Cachalot Lieutenant Commander G. A. Lewis
  Flying Fish Lieutenant Commander G. R. Donaho
  Tambor Lieutenant Commander J. W. Murphy
  Trout Lieutenant Commander F. W. Fenno
  Grayling Lieutenant Commander E. Olsen
  Nautilus Lieutenant Commander W. H. Brockman, Jr
  Grouper Lieutenant Commander C. E. Duke
  Dolphin Lieutenant Commander R. L. Rutter
  Gato Lieutenant Commander W. G. Myers
  Cuttlefish Lieutenant Commander M. P. Hottel
  Gudgeon Lieutenant Commander H. B. Lyon
  Grenadier Lieutenant Commander W. A. Lent
Roving Patrols
  Narwhal Lieutenant Commander C. W. Wilkins
  Plunger Lieutenant Commander D. C. White
  Trigger Lieutenant Commander J. H. Lewis
Local Patrol
  Tarpon Lieutenant Commander Lewis Wallace
  Pike Lieutenant Commander W. A. New
  Finback Lieutenant Commander J. L. Hull
  Growler Lieutenant Commander H. W. Gilmour

OTHER NAVAL UNITS

SEAPLANE TENDER FORCE – FRENCH FRIGATE SHOALS
Tenders
  Thornton Lieutenant Commander Wendell F. Kline
  Ballard Commander Myron T. Richardson
    (Both ex-destroyers: 1190 tons; 2 3in guns; 25 knots)
Destroyers
  Clark Commander Ward C. Gilbert (1850 tons; 8 5in guns;
    8 21in torpedoes; 37 knots)
Oiler
  Kaloli Lieutenant Commander G. H. Chapman, Jr (1729
    tons; ex-mercantile conversion)

Minesweeper
  Vireo (ATO) Lieutenant James C. Legg (840 tons; 2 3in guns; 14 knots)

MIDWAY RELIEF FUELLING UNIT: Commander Harry R. Thurber
Oiler
  Guadalupe Commander Thurber (7250 tons; 1 5in, 4 3in guns; 18 knots)
Destroyers
  Blue Commander Harold N. Williams
  Ralph Talbot Commander Ralph Earle, Jr (1500 tons; 4 5in guns; 16 21in torpedoes; 36 knots)

PQ17 – CONVOY TO HELL

by Paul Lund and Harry Ludlam

In June, 1942, Convoy PQ17, consisting of thirty-five merchant ships, set out for Russia with an escort of cruisers and destroyers. They had a reasonable chance of success until the order came to 'Scatter!'

What followed represents one of the most terrible and tragic blunders of the Second World War.

Authors Ludlam and Lund give a first hand account of the horror and despair that faced the men left to the mercy of a cruel enemy. From thousands of sources and recollections they have built up an unforgettable picture of what it was like to be in PQ17 – and survive...

NEW ENGLISH LIBRARY

NEL BESTSELLERS

Crime

T018 008	BUSMAN'S HONEYMOON	Dorothy L. Sayers 60p
T026 663	THE DOCUMENTS IN THE CASE	Dorothy L. Sayers 50p
T027 821	GAUDY NIGHT	Dorothy L. Sayers 75p
T030 180	UNNATURAL DEATH	Dorothy L. Sayers 60p
T026 671	FIVE RED HERRINGS	Dorothy L. Sayers 50p
T025 462	MURDER MUST ADVERTISE	Dorothy L. Sayers 50p

Fiction

T030 199	CRUSADER'S TOMB	A. J. Cronin £1.25
T029 522	HATTER'S CASTLE	A. J. Cronin £1.00
T027 228	THE SPANISH GARDNER	A. J. Cronin 45p
T013 936	THE JUDAS TREE	A. J. Cronin 50p
T015 386	THE NORTHERN LIGHT	A. J. Cronin 50p
T026 213	THE CITADEL	A. J. Cronin 80p
T027 112	BEYOND THIS PLACE	A. J. Cronin 60p
T016 609	KEYS OF THE KINGDOM	A. J. Cronin 60p
T029 158	THE STARS LOOK DOWN	A. J. Cronin £1.00
T022 021	THREE LOVES	A. J. Cronin 90p
T022 536	THE HARRAD EXPERIMENTS	Robert H. Rimmer 50p
T022 994	THE DREAM MERCHANTS	Harold Robbins 95p
T023 303	THE PIRATE	Harold Robbins 95p
T022 986	THE CARPETBAGGERS	Harold Robbins £1.00
T027 503	WHERE LOVE HAS GONE	Harold Robbins 90p
T023 958	THE ADVENTURERS	Harold Robbins £1.00
T025 241	THE INHERITORS	Harold Robbins 90p
T025 276	STILETTO	Harold Robbins 50p
T025 268	NEVER LEAVE ME	Harold Robbins 50p
T025 292	NEVER LOVE A STRANGER	Harold Robbins 90p
T022 226	A STONE FOR DANNY FISHER	Harold Robbins 80p
T025 284	79 PARK AVENUE	Harold Robbins 75p
T027 945	THE BETSY	Harold Robbins 90p
T029 557	RICH MAN, POOR MAN	Irwin Shaw £1.25
T017 532	EVENING IN BYZANTIUM	Irwin Shaw 60p
T021 025	THE MAN	Irving Wallace 90p
T020 916	THE PRIZE	Irving Wallace £1.00
T027 082	THE PLOT	Irving Wallace £1.00
T030 253	THE THREE SIRENS	Irving Wallace £1.25

Historical

T022 196	KNIGHT WITH ARMOUR	Alfred Duggan 50p
T022 250	THE LADY FOR RANSOM	Alfred Duggan 50p
T017 958	FOUNDING FATHERS	Alfred Duggan 50p
T022 625	LEOPARDS AND LILIES	Alfred Duggan 60p
T023 079	LORD GEOFFREY'S FANCY	Alfred Duggan 60p
T024 903	THE KING OF ATHELNEY	Alfred Duggan 60p
T020 169	FOX 9: CUT AND THRUST	Adam Hardy 30p
T021 300	FOX 10: BOARDER'S AWAY	Adam Hardy 35p
T023 125	FOX 11: FIRESHIP	Adam Hardy 35p
T024 946	FOX 12: BLOOD BEACH	Adam Hardy 35p

Science Fiction

T027 724	SCIENCE FICTION ART	Brian Aldiss £2.95
T030 245	TIME ENOUGH FOR LOVE	Robert Heinlein £1.25
T029 492	STRANGER IN A STRANGE LAND	Robert Heinlein 80p
T029 484	I WILL FEAR NO EVIL	Robert Heinlein 95p
T026 817	THE HEAVEN MAKERS	Frank Herbert 35p
T027 279	DUNE	Frank Herbert 90p
T022 854	DUNE MESSIAH	Frank Herbert 60p
T023 974	THE GREEN BRAIN	Frank Herbert 35p
T015 270	THE WEAPON MAKERS	A. E. Van Vogt 30p
T023 265	EMPIRE OF THE ATOM	A. E. Van Vogt 40p
T027 473	THE FAR OUT WORLD OF A. E. VAN VOGT	
		A. E. Van Vogt 50p

War

T027 066	COLDITZ: THE GERMAN STORY	*Reinhold Eggers* 50p
T020 827	COLDITZ RECAPTURED	*Reinhold Eggers* 50p
T020 584	THE GOOD SHEPHERD	*C. S. Forester* 40p
T012 999	PQ 17 – CONVOY TO HELL	*Lund & Ludlam* 30p
T026 299	TRAWLERS GO TO WAR	*Lund & Ludlam* 50p
T025 438	LILLIPUT FLEET	*A. Cecil Hampshire* 50p
T020 495	ILLUSTRIOUS	*Kenneth Poolman* 40p
T018 032	ARK ROYAL	*Kenneth Poolman* 40p
T027 198	THE GREEN BERET	*Hilary St George Saunders* 50p
T027 171	THE RED BERET	*Hilary St George Saunders* 50p

Western

T017 893	EDGE 12: THE BIGGEST BOUNTY	*George Gilman* 30p
T023 931	EDGE 13: A TOWN CALLED HATE	*George Gilman* 35p
T020 002	EDGE 14: THE BIG GOLD	*George Gilman* 30p
T020 754	EDGE 15: BLOOD RUN	*George Gilman* 35p
T022 706	EDGE 16: THE FINAL SHOT	*George Gilman* 35p
T024 881	EDGE 17: VENGEANCE VALLEY	*George Gilman* 40p
T026 604	EDGE 18: TEN TOMBSTONES TO TEXAS	*George Gilman* 40p
T028 135	EDGE 19: ASHES AND DUST	*George Gilman* 40p

General

T017 400	CHOPPER	*Peter Cave* 30p
T022 838	MAMA	*Peter Cave* 35p
T021 009	SEX MANNERS FOR MEN	*Robert Chartham* 35p
T023 206	THE BOOK OF LOVE	*Dr David Delvin* 90p
T028 623	CAREFREE LOVE	*Dr David Delvin* 60p

Mad

S006 739	MADVERTISING	70p
S006 292	MORE SNAPPY ANSWERS TO STUPID QUESTIONS	70p
S006 245	VOODOO MAD	70p
S006 741	MAD POWER	70p
S006 291	HOPPING MAD	70p

NEL P.O. BOX 11, FALMOUTH, TR10 9EN, CORNWALL.

For U.K.: Customers should include to cover postage, 18p for the first book plus 8p per copy for each additional book ordered up to a maximum charge of 66p.

For B.F.P.O. and Eire: Customers should include to cover postage, 18p for the first book plus 8p per copy for the next 6 and thereafter 3p per book.

For Overseas: Customers should include to cover postage, 20p for the first book plus 10p per copy for each additional book.

Name ....

Address..

....

....

Title ....
(JULY)

Whilst every effort is made to maintain prices, new editions or printings may carry an increased price and the actual price of the edition supplied will apply.